FEAR and ANXIETY
IN DOGS

UNDERSTANDING, PREVENTION AND TREATMENT

FEAR and ANXIETY IN DOGS

UNDERSTANDING, PREVENTION AND TREATMENT

Caroline Clark

THE CROWOOD PRESS

First published in 2022 by
The Crowood Press Ltd
Ramsbury, Marlborough
Wiltshire SN8 2HR

enquiries@crowood.com
www.crowood.com

This impression 2024

British Library Cataloguing-in-Publication Data
A catalogue record for this book is available from the British Library.

ISBN 978 0 71984112 5

Cover design by Sergey Tsvetkov
Cover photograph by Tommy Taylor

Frontispiece: Caroline and Millie. (Photo: Tommy Taylor)

Dedication
This book is dedicated to Robbie, Holly and Lily whose paw prints will remain on my heart forever.

Typeset by Simon and Sons

Printed and bound in India by Replika Press Pvt. Ltd.

Contents

Introduction

If you have already bought this book, thank you, or have been attracted by the title to pick it up, then I'm guessing that you own or work with a dog(s) that suffers from fear and anxiety. If that's the case, you have just taken a crucial step towards helping them change their lives forever.

In my work as a clinical animal behaviourist, canine fear and anxiety-related problems make up a large proportion of my caseload, so I know how damaging they can be. Life for the dog is often miserable and distressing and owners are usually at their wits' end, feeling frustrated, upset and confused. But with the right sort of help and advice, things can improve.

The good news is that dogs don't have to spend their lives feeling frightened and anxious. We can influence their behaviour by guiding them and managing the triggers that prompt their fear. We can help them access coping strategies and, through positive reinforcement, we can teach them alternative behaviours that feel good and are incompatible with fear and anxiety. How to accomplish all that and formulate an integrated and holistic treatment plan for them is right here, in this book.

The book is split up into two main sections. The first part is designed to help you understand what is actually going on. We look inside the dog's brain and see the effects that fear and anxiety have on their body, helping us appreciate why a dog may be finding it difficult to control the way they behave. We also delve into the various factors that influence the development of fear and anxiety and consider ways to prevent it. Making sense of canine communication is crucial for interpreting a dog's emotional state and, for this reason, a chapter has been devoted to the messages a dog is trying to convey. Aggression, frustration and reactivity are some of the most challenging behaviours to understand. However, difficult dogs are usually distressed dogs and so I have included relevant information and practical solutions for dealing with these problems too.

The second half of the book draws on what has been learned in the first part and is concerned with analysing behaviour, training techniques and treatment methods. A range of commonly encountered problems are included in the form of case studies and these provide the reader with comprehensive and proven treatment options which can be used as a base for tackling other similar problems. Step-by-step illustrated training guides are also included to help consolidate the information.

You'll get the most out of this book by reading each section in order, as the earlier chapters act as a platform for information and ideas introduced later on. However, you may prefer to dip in and out of it, which is why I have interspersed it with tables, feature boxes and short stories about real-life cases.

PART ONE

Understanding Fear and Anxiety: Making Sense of It All

CHAPTER 1

What's Going On?

Definitions of and Differences between Fear, Anxiety, Phobia and Stress

Fear and anxiety are emotions that underlie some of the most challenging and problematic canine behaviours. Problems including separation anxiety, fear of sudden noises and fear-aggression towards unfamiliar dogs are just a few examples. Nevertheless, before focusing in on the problem it is important to consider what these emotions mean for the dog and to understand the physiological forces and processes that drive and maintain their behaviour. Having this sort of knowledge not only enables us to gain some insight into what is actually going on internally, it also provides us with a much greater sense of empathy for their plight.

Terms such as fear, anxiety, phobia and stress are often used interchangeably. However, although they share some features and give rise to similar outward signs, they do have different meanings. Therefore, to avoid confusion, it is useful to have a clear definition of what they all actually mean and to know something about each of them. So let's see what is really going on below the surface…

What is Fear?

When fear is in proportion to the danger, it is a normal, adaptive response, essential for survival. Without it, and the reactions that it triggers, animals would be extremely vulnerable. It makes perfect sense therefore, to act fearfully to something that is known or perceived to

OPPOSITE: Pinky, courtesy of Dawn Chapman.

be dangerous. Nevertheless, it becomes damaging when it is disproportionate to the situation or when the fear response is continually triggered by non-threatening stimuli and the dog spends a large proportion of its time being in a state of fear.

A key feature of fear is that it is directed to the location or object of the fearful stimulus and the fear response is terminated when the object of fear is removed. So, for example, a dog that is frightened of going to the vets will react when they are in the veterinary clinic, and in the presence of the vet, but the fearful response will stop when they are removed from that situation.

For some dogs, the consequences of fear can be far reaching and affect their quality of life. This is the case for those that exhibit fearfulness to everyday events and objects that are difficult to avoid such as traffic, other dogs and strangers. This makes life miserable for them and difficult for an owner to manage. Some dogs might be fearful of a specific circumstance such as being left alone, as is the case in separation anxiety, or of noises such as fireworks or thunderstorms. Extreme fear responses can be difficult to control and, in some cases, can cause clinical effects such as diarrhoea, vomiting and changes in appetite.

Fearfulness in dogs can be categorized as social and non-social fearfulness (Table 1.1).

What is Anxiety?

Anxiety is the anticipation of a fearful event, sometimes described as apprehensive expectation. In other words, the dog is waiting for something frightening and unpleasant to occur rather than reacting to a specific stimulus. Anxious dogs can spend large amounts of time worrying and are often in a state of hypervigilance: scanning

Table 1.1. Examples and differences between social fear and non-social fear.

Social Fear (animate things and social situations)	Non-social Fear (inanimate things)
Familiar people Strangers Children Dogs Other animals Visits to the vet Trips to the grooming parlour Being touched and handled	Noises Thunderstorms/fireworks (sounds and flashing lights) Traffic Bicycles Umbrellas Wheelchairs Prams Scents, such as disinfectants or smoke Tactile triggers, such as tiles or slippery floor surfaces Crates

their environment and startling easily. Chronic anxiety is physically and mentally tiring and serves no real function. Therefore, it is actually considered abnormal and is a recognized welfare concern.

Generalized anxiety disorder (GAD) is a well-known condition in humans but it can affect dogs and other animals too. People with GAD report restlessness and irritability and constant worry interferes with their daily life. All these symptoms are likely to correspond to how an anxious dog presents and, although we can't ask them, this insight helps us gain some idea of how they might be feeling.

Despite the differences, fear and anxiety can occur together and sometimes the signs overlap. Indeed, it is often very hard to pick the two apart because we can't ask the dog if they are worrying about something specific and in the present or whether they are worrying in anticipation of something that might happen in the future. Because of this cross-over, and not always knowing what the dog actually does feel, these two emotional states are often considered to be on the same scope.

What is Phobia?

Phobia is an extreme and intense fear reaction and, unlike fear, can persist long after the event is over. It is usually associated with something that isn't in itself considered dangerous, at least not to the unaffected party. Nevertheless, this non-dangerous thing (for example the sound of thunder, fireworks or being left alone) causes an extreme and irrational panic response, just as if the dog was in mortal danger. A phobic reaction usually escalates quickly and limits the dog's ability to behave normally. Some dogs with severe separation-related

issues or sonophobia (extreme fear of noises) have been known to tear down a wall or chew through a door to escape, often causing trauma and injury to themselves in the process.

Being aware of the distinct differences between fear, anxiety and phobia is useful for accurately diagnosing a problem and guides the direction of how a case is managed and treated. Nevertheless, because they share similar physiological signs, they are often collectively referred to as fear-related problems.

Recognizing the Signs

When a dog is frightened or anxious they display a wide range of body signals and behavioural signs. A number of these are evident as whole-body postures although facial expressions can also convey fearful emotions, including tension around the jaw line, dilated pupils and alterations in the ear position.

Another feature of fear is the **fear-potentiated-startle response**. This makes the dog more on edge. In this state they become much more likely to startle at small noises or movements. It's the same phenomenon that some of us might experience after we have been watching a scary film and are on high alert and easily surprised. Under the influence of these emotions, there can be a danger that a dog will redirect their fear and bite someone if they make a sudden appearance or unexpectedly touch them.

What is Stress?

Stress is the broad term used to describe the changes that cause behavioural, emotional and psychological strain in response to difficult or fear-provoking situations. Strictly speaking, in the biological sense, stress that is perceived

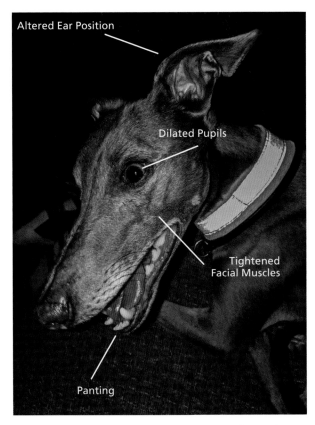

Altered Ear Position

Dilated Pupils

Tightened Facial Muscles

Panting

An extremely frightened greyhound during a firework event displaying a number of fearful facial expressions. (Photo: Morris, courtesy of Sarah Kitching)

Signs of Canine Fear, Anxiety and Stress

A dog may show one or a combination of any of the following signals:

- Alterations in the ear position (lowered and flattened to the head or tense and upright)
- Alterations in tail posture – usually tucked close to the anus
- Baring the teeth
- Cowering, crouching and cringing
- Dilated pupils (widening of the pupils)
- Easily startled
- Excessive salivation (drooling)
- Furrowed brow
- Hiding
- Hypervigilance (on high alert)
- Licking and chomping
- Lunging towards the object of fear
- Narrowing the eyes
- Raised hackles (piloerection)
- Rapid eye blinks
- Stiffening of the body
- Snapping
- Tension in the muscles of the body and tightness around the face and jaw
- Trembling and shaking
- Turning the head or body away
- Urinating and defecating in fear
- Vocalizing, for example whining, whimpering, barking, growling
- Yawning

as being bad or negative is called 'distress' and stress that is perceived as being positive and useful is known as 'eustress'. Eustress might be the short-term excitement a dog feels before completing an agility course or could be evident in a hunting dog when pursuing quarry. Eustress enhances performance and is a normal, healthy state. However, in this book, I shall largely use the terms stress and distress interchangeably.

Stress can be described as acute or chronic:

- Acute stress is short-lived and the body quickly recovers with no long-term damage.
- Chronic stress is persistent, prolonged and constantly recurs. This is the most physically and emotionally damaging.

The events, experiences and sensations that underlie and trigger stress are called **stressors** (Fig. 1.1). Depending on the dog's temperament and experience, a stressor can include something seemingly minor (to us) through to something more obviously frightening and threatening.

As with the human experience, a dog's life is filled with a range of unavoidable stressors. These might include everyday occurrences such as meeting new people and other dogs or visiting new places. Dogs bred from stable parents, with appropriate early exposure and positive experiences to these situations, usually take them all in their stride and recover rapidly. Unfortunately, some dogs are unable to cope and overreact to stressors,

Cowering is a common body posture exhibited in anxious and fearful dogs. (Photo: Oliver, courtesy of Amy Clark)

An anxious dog displaying a furrowed brow, licking and dilated pupils. (Photo: Bella, courtesy of Sadie Fox)

Fig. 1.1. Anything that triggers a stress response is called a stressor.

leading to a punishing daily struggle and regularly triggering what is called the **stress response,** also known as the fight-or-flight reaction.

The Stress Response (Fight-or-Flight Reaction)

The **stress response** evolved as a survival mechanism and has a critical role in preparing an animal for real threat. However, for the fearful and anxious dog, this response often remains activated and in charge for a large part of their time budget.

Put simply, during a frightening situation, the dog receives information from the outside world via their main senses. From there, specialized neurones (nerves) send information to a part of the brain called the amygdala (more of that soon), where it is processed and interpreted. Once the alarm is raised another brain structure, called the hypothalamus, co-ordinates a multi-action process, preparing the dog to deal with the danger at hand.

Immediately, a specialized part of the nervous system called the autonomic nervous system (ANS) is activated. The ANS controls involuntary actions (things outside the dog's control) such as blood flow, heartbeat and breathing. A branch of this that is responsible for speeding up these actions (known as the sympathetic nervous system) is then called in to play.

In response, the heartbeat and pulse quicken, breathing becomes more rapid and the adrenal glands (two structures located above the kidneys) release stress hormones.

The three major stress hormones include:

- Epinephrine (also known as adrenaline)
- Norepinephrine (also known as noradrenaline)
- Cortisol

Within seconds epinephrine and norepinephrine flood through the system bringing a number of physiological changes. These are all designed to hone the dog's senses, to help them fight off an opponent or to run away and take flight in order to survive (Table 1.2). Hence the term 'fight-or-flight reaction'. Examples of these survival mechanisms are evident when a frightened dog bolts after being scared or when it lunges, snaps and bites if threatened.

Table 1.2. Examples of the effects of epinephrine and norepinephrine during the stress response.

Organs and Body Systems Affected	Physiological Effects of Epinephrine and Norepinephrine	The Function
Heart	• Increases the rate and force of contraction, increasing the output of blood and raising blood pressure.	• To prepare the body for strenuous activity.
Circulation	• Diverts blood flow to the brain, large muscles and lungs. • Decreases the flow of blood to the digestive system, the skin and the peripheral parts of the body.	• Blood delivers oxygen and energy supplies to the brain in order to enhance alertness. • Blood diverted to large muscles and the lungs prepare for flight and fight. • Digestion and blood flow to the skin and extremities is slowed down so that the body can divert all its internal energy to dealing with the perceived danger at hand.
Lungs	• Increased respiration and dilation of bronchioles (tiny passageways in the lung).	• To help increase and maintain oxygen supplies.
The eye	• Dilates pupils.	• To allow more light to enter the eyes, improving vision and the ability to scan the surroundings.

The term 'fight-or-flight' reaction was first coined by the American psychologist Walter Bradford Cannon somewhere around 1915. However, as our knowledge has increased, we now know that as part of the stress response, other reactions come in to play, more commonly called the freeze and fiddle (or flail) reactions.

The freeze response involves a dog becoming motionless or making extremely slow, creeping movements, sometimes taking cover until the danger has passed. Others just pin themselves to the ground and lay low, hoping they have not been seen and will be left alone. Conversely, some dogs will just fiddle or flail around, not quite knowing how to respond. This reaction can sometimes be missed but is often demonstrated when dogs are being physically restrained for veterinary examinations, when being groomed or other similar procedures.

What does cortisol do?

After the initial surge of epinephrine and norepinephrine, cortisol is then released. As well as fuelling the stress response, cortisol plays an important role in managing how the body uses carbohydrates, fats and proteins. It also regulates blood pressure and increases glucose in the bloodstream, providing an energy boost which is required for ongoing danger.

Like epinephrine and norepinephrine, cortisol can curb bodily functions that would be non-essential or even detrimental in a fight-and-flight situation. Systems such as digestion, reproduction, immune responses and even growth processes can be switched off until the threat is over so that energy can be re-directed to the more important body systems required for survival.

All the effects that result in the stress response are part of a finely tuned process and, in normal circumstances, after the danger has passed, these body processes calm down and the dog returns to its normal baseline state. Yet, if a dog remains under constant stress and the alarm button stays on, this disruption can eventually lead to physical and psychological health issues.

Cortisol is sometimes measured in the bloodstream, saliva, hair and urine to determine stress levels in the body. Baseline readings are measured against samples taken to assess the magnitude of change.

The Brain and Behaviour

The limbic system is the part of the brain that is responsible for processing information and for behavioural and emotional responses. Two structures of particular significance are the amygdala and the hippocampus (Fig. 1.2).

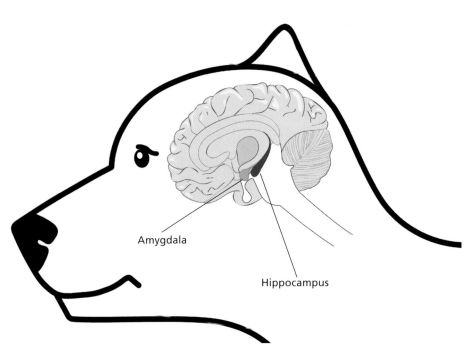

Amygdala

Hippocampus

Fig. 1.2. The position of the amygdala and hippocampus in the brain.

The **amygdala** is responsible for controlling the way dogs (and other mammals) recognize, process and express emotions like fear and anxiety and, as previously mentioned, has a role to play in the stress response. The amygdala determines how deeply the memory of an emotional experience is stored and, unsurprisingly, memories linked to fear and trauma tend to become more deeply rooted.

The **hippocampus** is adjacent to the amygdala and is also responsible for memory formation, although, whereas the amygdala stores the memories of traumatic experiences, the hippocampus plays a part in linking sensations to the memory.

It makes complete sense for any animal to remember something that was frightening and recall it quickly so it can take rapid action to avoid it next time. For this reason, fearful memories can be formed after only a few repetitions and sometimes, if distressing enough, just one event is all that is required for them to learn something from their experience. This is called single-event or one-event learning.

Murphy's story demonstrates how a single, traumatic incident can quickly become lodged in a dog's memory

Murphy's Single-Event Learning Experience

Murphy was a sixteen-week-old Labrador puppy when he was taken out for a walk with his owner on a narrow pavement, alongside a main road. Suddenly, a very large, noisy, articulated lorry thundered past him. Murphy bolted in the opposite direction towards a hedge that lined the pavement to try and hide. The next day, when getting him ready to go out, he seemed nervous when his owner tried to put on his harness and lead but she didn't think much of it. Upon reaching the location where the frightening experience took place, Murphy was reluctant to move forward and put on the brakes. However, the worst reaction was when he saw a lorry coming along the road towards him. Murphy went into a complete meltdown, spinning on the lead and desperately trying to move in the opposite direction. Clearly he'd learned by just that one previous frightening event that going for a walk represented danger and that lorries were to be avoided at all costs.

and how this kind of experience can lead to the development of future problems. It also provides a neat example of something called fear conditioning. Because conditioning is often used as another word for learning, it also goes by the name of fear learning.

Fear conditioning is a simple form of associative learning, occurring when a neutral stimulus (something not frightening in itself) has been paired with an aversive fear-eliciting stimulus such as pain, a loud startling noise or any other traumatic experience. In Murphy's story, the neutral stimulus was the lorry but when it was paired with the loud noise it made, and the motion of it coming towards him, negative associations were rapidly formed. Fear conditioning can also become associated with the context or in the set of circumstances related to an event. This is called contextual fear conditioning and explains why Murphy was nervous when he saw the harness and lead, and why fearful emotions were triggered when he returned to the location where he experienced the trauma.

Another phenomenon that can complicate matters even further is called fear generalization. This is when fear responses begin to extend to other things and scenarios that appear similar to the original frightening trigger. Through this, Murphy may begin to generalize the sound and sight of a lorry to the sound of other large vehicles and, over time, may become fearful of all traffic.

Neurotransmitters

Another way that the brain mobilizes activity in response to stress is through neurotransmitters. In common with stress hormones, neurotransmitters are chemical messengers but they work by sending their messages between neurons (nerve cells) targeting cells all over the body. Because epinephrine and norepinephrine also have a role in helping neurones communicate, they can be categorized as neurotransmitters as well as hormones.

In addition to other roles within the body, certain neurotransmitters play an important part in the brain systems that regulate mood and emotional behaviour. Consequently, disruptions to their production have been linked with fear-related problems.

Three neurotransmitters of particular significance include:

- Serotonin (sometimes called the happy hormone)
- Gamma aminobutyric acid (GABA)
- Dopamine

In accord with one another, the production of these neurotransmitters can be increased through naturally pleasing activities including exercise, play, and mental enrichment.

Serotonin is scientifically known as 5-hydroxy-tryptamine, often abbreviated to 5-HT. As well as its effect on feelings of well-being, it also has roles in regulating sleep and appetite. Studies in the field of canine behaviour have suggested that lower levels are linked with aggression and impulsivity.

GABA is instrumental in reducing stress, lowering anxiety, and creating a calm mood. GABA is often found as a listed ingredient in a number of natural, over-the-counter canine calming supplements.

Dopamine is involved in working memory, focus, attention and motivation. Sleep deprivation and stress can reduce dopamine levels and this may lead to a downward spiral of events, contributing to the maintenance of fear-related problems. Dopamine spikes when an animal receives or anticipates receiving a pleasurable reward, which is why positive reinforcement training should be an important feature of a treatment plan. Another extremely effective way of inducing the release of dopamine naturally is through the seeking system. Therefore, incorporating activities based on 'seek and find' and scent work is recommended.

Coping Strategies

How a dog responds and copes with a frightening or stressful event can be determined by genetics, previous experience and their behavioural profile. However, dogs tend to deal with a situation in a much better way if we can provide them with a sense of choice, control and freedom to access their coping strategies.

Coping Styles

Depending on the individual and the environmental context, there is some variation in a dog's coping style. Instinctively, a dog's primary response is avoidance. This includes backing off, escaping and/or finding somewhere to hide and retreat. Some dogs cope by using aggressive behaviours although, in the wild, injuries through fighting would have, at best, been painful and, at worst, proved fatal. So, for this reason, avoidance is usually favoured. Nevertheless, if a dog is unable to escape the source of fear, they may well use aggression (fight).

Providing a dog with something safe to chew can help relieve stress. (Photo: Ruby, courtesy of Karen Taylor)

Some of the ways a dog expresses fear mirror their species-specific coping strategies. For example, behaviours such as pacing might be associated with flight and seeking a safe refuge. Vocalizing might be a way of trying to communicate with the social group for back-up and support, while digging and destruction is most probably linked to hiding and escape. Chewing has also been shown to have a stress coping function and this may explain why some dogs resort to chewing furniture and other items when they are under stress. Providing them with an outlet, by means of a safe toy or edible chew, is therefore a good idea.

Creating a Safe Refuge

In the wild, a place of safety would probably be beneath some undergrowth in a darkened place. Here the dog would nestle down and hide until it was safe to emerge. Domestic dogs often take similar action but, without the necessary means, they will often try and find somewhere that provides them with the same sense of protection. Some can be driven to seemingly inappropriate behaviours such as digging the stuffing from a sofa in a bid to escape whereas others might choose to hide under or behind furniture. Unless a dog is going to injure themselves or cause damage, it is better to leave them there. Pulling them out will only add to their fear and make them feel more vulnerable.

One way of helping them out is to create a den, preferably somewhere they show a preference for retreating. The den should provide them with all the features that mimic a natural hide, such as a quiet location, low-level lighting and a sense of being hidden.

Hiding and avoidance behaviours are common canine coping strategies. (Photo: Woody, courtesy of Debby Richmond)

Open crates can provide somewhere accessible for a dog to take refuge during frightening events. (Photo: Darcey, courtesy of Lora Lane)

Providing a Dog with a Sense of Control

When a dog feels scared, problems invariably worsen if they have no opportunity to take action. Being restrained on a lead, cornered or confined can induce panic. Using crates inappropriately can also generate fear. When a dog is properly trained, they can become a safe haven but not if the dog is shut in and feels trapped, especially during a frightening event.

Obviously safety is important and allowing a dog to have complete freedom is not always an option when outside the home. But we can help them feel a sense of control by removing them or putting distance between them and the target of their fear. Similarly when working with dogs that emit a fearful response, let's say in a veterinary environment or grooming parlour, just backing off, stopping what we are doing and thinking about other ways to approach a certain procedure can rapidly diffuse a situation and instantly make the dog feel better.

Comforting a Frightened Dog

Throughout the thousands of years of domestication, dogs have developed a close alliance with humans. Because of this bond, many dogs rely on their owners as a secure base, turning to them when frightened. In this sense, the owner's presence can be deemed part of the coping mechanism for some dogs. Unfortunately, there is a widely propagated myth that giving comfort and soothing a frightened dog can somehow reinforce their fearfulness, causing the fear to worsen. This is not the case. In the first place, fear is a natural emotion and so cannot be conditioned and secondly, ignoring a dog when it is feeling vulnerable isn't going to help them feel less distressed. To illustrate this point, imagine that you have been involved in car accident and you're pretty shaken up. Would being offered sympathy and comfort make you feel more frightened? And how would you feel if you were ignored? Probably worse. So offering security and calm reassurance is fine. Nonetheless, it is important

17

The owner's presence can be comforting during a frightening experience. (Photo: Coco, courtesy of Danielle Kennedy)

Habituation is the earliest and most simple form of learning. In the context of puppy development it's about teaching a puppy what to ignore and what not to be concerned about and this is done through repetition and sensitive exposure to lots of different stimuli. Over time the puppy learns that certain things that they regularly hear, touch, see and smell are just part of their day-to-day environment and are not to be feared or attended to.

Socialization is a process where the puppy learns how to interact with other dogs, animals, people and situations within a social context. The critical time frame for socialization starts at around three weeks of age and runs until they are about twelve to fourteen weeks old. During this time it's important to expose a puppy carefully and positively to all the things they might encounter throughout their adult life.

to ensure the kind of attention being given isn't making the dog worse so I usually advise owners to monitor their dog's response to make sure that the right level of support is being provided.

Common Presentations of Fear-Related Problems

Fear-related problems can manifest in numerous ways although some of the most common presentations include:

- Fear of loud, sudden noises
- Separation anxiety disorders
- Fear of people/strangers
- Fear of other dogs
- Fear of inanimate objects (for example prams, umbrellas, bicycles and traffic)
- Fear of the veterinarian and the veterinary clinic
- Generalized Anxiety Disorder

There are a number of reasons why and how these behaviour problems develop and we shall be exploring some of these later in the book. However, a common theme

is inadequate habituation and socialization. Without undergoing these processes, the young dog is unprepared for life experiences and is unable to cope with everyday stressors.

Basic and Immediate Help for Fear-Related Problems

We shall be exploring the treatment protocols for some common fear-related problems in Part II of the book. However, immediate treatment focuses on the welfare of the dog and on health and safety. As a general guide the following steps should be taken:

- Stop forcing the dog to face its fears.
- Identify things that trigger the behaviour and avoid exposure to them.
- Stop any form of punishment as this heightens fear and can lead to fear-aggression (even shouting at a dog is a form of punishment).
- Create a safe and calm environment (for example a den).
- Follow health and safety measures, such as securing boundaries, carrying out muzzle training.
- Contact a veterinary surgeon to rule out any pain or medical problems.

- Seek the help of a suitably qualified canine behaviour counsellor.

Other early measures include making a list of the triggers and, wherever possible, removing the dog from them or at least reducing their exposure to them. This is because repeated negative experiences can cause something called behavioural sensitization, sometimes referred to as reverse tolerance.

Behavioural sensitization occurs with repeated exposure to an aversive stimulus. An example of this might be if a dog was subjected to an extremely loud noise. The effect would cause the dog to be more on edge, agitated and more highly reactive to other things going on in the environment. For this reason, the dog should not be made to face its fears, nor should they be chastised.

Encouraging calmness can help to mitigate some of the effects of stress and therefore other first-line strategies might include the administration of natural calming supplements, performing relaxing massage techniques and introducing scent or pheromone therapies.

Once the dog is in a better emotional state, work can begin on a targeted behaviour modification plan under the guidance of a suitably qualified behaviour counsellor.

Fear of Loud and Sudden Noises

While some dogs show fear towards everyday noises like traffic, the vacuum cleaner or other indoor appliances, it is mostly sudden, intermittent and sporadic loud noises that provoke the most dramatic fear responses. Some of the most common and frequently reported are unpredictable events such as thunderstorms, fireworks, gunshots and bird-scarers. Alarms can be painfully loud and can trigger generalized anxieties or separation-related disorders if one suddenly goes off when the dog is alone.

In common with other fear-related problems, noise sensitivities can be based on poor habituation and socialization or they may have been triggered by a frightening experience. Being taken to a firework event, where the dog was overwhelmed by the sound and sights of the display, experiencing a sudden thunderstorm when they were in a conservatory (which would act as a sound-box and include lots of visual stimulation) and being startled by the sudden blast of a nearby gunshot whilst on a walk in the countryside are all examples of cases that I have been involved with.

As we have seen, dogs form memories of fearful situations quickly and can learn by making associations with other things that are going on at the same time. Making connections with darkening skies and detecting changes in barometric pressure prior to a thunderstorm, becoming fearful of walks in the countryside after experiencing the sound of gunshots in that setting and picking up the smell of smoke from a fire because of the association it had with a firework event are all examples. These other environmental stimuli begin to predict that something frightening is going to happen even if most of the time they don't. As time passes, the original source of fear can therefore become hidden, making it difficult to make sense of what is going on.

'Fear generalization' can be another complicating factor and so the sound of thunder might generalize to the sound of the tumble drier, a car backfiring or even a door slamming.

Fear of People and Strangers

Fear of people and strangers can simply be because the person is unknown to the dog and therefore they have no knowledge of whether they pose a threat or not. At other times, fears may be based on a previous negative experience involving a person and the dog subsequently goes on to generalize their fear to others who have a similar appearance. However, lack of exposure to a wide range of people during the dog's socialization period is often at the root of the problem.

Dogs tend to show a greater fear response towards males when compared to females, perhaps because men are generally of a larger build and have a deeper tone of voice. Children and babies can also provoke fear, most likely because they communicate differently to adults. Children and babies tend to shout, scream, crawl and make uncoordinated movements and this, along with well-intended but clumsy interactions, is probably why young children are bitten more than any other family member.

In contrast, some dogs are just fearful of people coming to the door or inside the home. Unfortunately, it's not uncommon for ill-informed owners to use a crate to help their dog overcome fearfulness of visitors and, in a bid to desensitize them, they shut the dog inside whilst the visitor is invited in to the same room. Alas, without a means of escape, this is more likely to increase the dog's fear.

Anything new or strange, like someone wearing a hat, motorbike helmet or high-visibility clothing might be a trigger and fast movement, such as joggers and people riding bicycles or skateboards, can also prompt a fear reaction.

It can be difficult for people to understand why a dog may appear fine with some people and less so with others. When trying to explain to clients, I often use the analogy of us seeing an alien walking down the street. Although they may appear as a human form, something about them is very different. Having no previous experience of meeting an alien from outer space or anything that looks like them makes them seem sinister and frightening and we wouldn't know if they were friend or foe. In a similar way, anything that the dog has never encountered before or isn't the norm is bound to cause alarm. A significant part of being able to help a dog therefore begins with analysing whether it is all people they are fearful of or whether it is possible to pinpoint what it is about the person that evokes a fearful response. Once this has been established a targeted treatment plan can be designed.

Fear of Other Dogs

Fear of other dogs can be one of the most frustrating canine problems, turning a pleasant dog walk into a distressing event for both the dog and their owner. The motivation for this behaviour can be similar to the development of fears of people in terms of a previous, negative experience. Some dogs may go on to develop a problem after being attacked or frightened by another dog, which may lead to a fear of a particular type or breed of dog. Yet, this might generalize towards dogs of all descriptions as time goes on. Inadequate or a complete lack of socialization with other dogs is another extremely common reason for this problem, which is why socializing dogs properly and encouraging them to meet and interact with a range of other dogs during the critical time frame is crucial.

As with all behaviour problems, treatment relies on thorough analysis. Reflecting on how and when the problem began and making observations to determine whether it is all dogs that evoke a response or whether it is a particular type of dog (or perhaps the person walking them) that is the trigger.

Fear of Inanimate Objects

Absolutely anything could induce fear; common causes include bicycles, traffic, prams and wheelchairs. Mostly it's the sight of the thing that causes a response although the noise the object makes, its smell and how it feels can also be triggers. For example, the smell of surgical spirit may generate the memory of being at the vets and some dogs are fearful of slippery floors if they haven't ever experienced walking on them before or have slipped and injured themselves in the past.

Things that are novel and may never have been seen before, such as kites and hot-air balloons can be especially frightening. However, dog crates that have been associated with their confinement or objects that have inflicted pain, accidently or knowingly, are other potential stimuli. Teasing out this kind of information, and finding out what it is about the stimulus that elicits the fear, is all part of behavioural analysis, a topic we shall be looking at in more depth in Part II.

Separation Anxiety (SA) Disorders

As a species, humans tend to have a desire to give and receive attention. Of course our dogs deserve that too. However, if we are not careful, we can unwittingly cause dogs to rely on our presence, and engender hyper-attachment (having a particularly strong bond to the owner or attachment figure), which can lead to separation anxiety.

Hyper-attachment isn't the only reason a dog becomes distressed when left alone, as shown in Table 1.3.

Table 1.3. Other motivating factors implicated in separation anxiety disorders.

Factors	Comments
Fear of being trapped	Common in dogs that are kept in confined spaces or crates without undergoing the proper training.
Anxiety about the owner's return in anticipation of being punished	This can occur if a dog has been punished for causing destruction or soiling the house. The dog then begins to anticipate their owner's return with trepidation.
Poor habituation to solitude	Never being taught or having experienced being left alone.
Associating being left alone with a frightening event	Examples include: the burglar or smoke alarm going off, the window cleaner suddenly appearing at the window or unusual and frightening noises from outside, such as roadworks.
Boredom	Destruction and chewing mistaken for anxiety.

Consequently, exploring the underlying cause, rather than viewing SA as a single problem, is a key factor in achieving a successful outcome.

Signs of separation anxiety (SA) disorders

Signs are varied and, depending on the severity of the problem, range from mild distress to phobic reactions. Some of the signs include:

- Unnecessary seeking of reassurance whilst the owner is present.
- Shadowing the owner and anxiously following them around when they anticipate them leaving.
- Signs of anxiety when the owner is departing or at their departure cues, for example putting outside garments on, picking up keys, hearing the car drive away.
- Over enthusiastic greetings (sometimes frenzied).
- Destruction (often focused on escape).
- Inability to rest and settle when left alone.
- Pacing and panting.
- Salivating.
- Defaecation and urination.
- Distress vocalization.
- Vomiting and diarrhoea.

SA can be categorized as:

1. **Mild:** The dog is clingy and shows mild anxiety when left but they are able to sleep and settle between episodes of anxiety. However, mild cases can develop into more serious forms if not addressed promptly.
2. **Moderate:** The dog shadows the owner and they find it difficult to rest and settle when alone. Greetings when the owner returns are frenzied.
3. **Severe:** Severe forms of separation anxiety are challenging. Symptoms are varied and can include any of the aforementioned. However, salivation, loss of bladder and bowel control, vomiting and diarrhoea, constant pacing, destruction and a complete inability to relax when left alone may manifest.

The overriding emotions for dogs with separation anxiety are combinations of anxiety, fear and in extreme situations phobia. Phobic reactions usually result in the dog self-harming and, in an attempt to escape, they can cause major destruction in the home.

Dogs with SA will often chew items and cause damage to exit points. Note damage to skirting boards and the door frame. (Photo: Zara, courtesy of Amanda Dobbs)

Unfortunately, there is no quick fix for this problem and, because SA can be one of the more challenging behaviour problems to diagnose and treat, it is advisable to seek the help of an experienced and suitably qualified animal behaviourist as soon as possible.

Fear of the Veterinarian and Trips to the Veterinary Clinic

Most dogs rapidly form a negative association with the vet and the veterinary clinic from a young age. Unfortunately, for most puppies, their first visit is to receive their vaccinations and to be microchipped and, for some, this can be a painful and distressing experience. Subsequent visits tend to be when the dog is ill, injured or undergoing medical and surgical procedures, where they have to be separated from the owner, which adds another dimension to their distress. Consequently, their fear develops further.

Positive experiences within a veterinary clinic during a puppy's socialization period can make future trips there much less stressful. (Photo: Myrtle, courtesy of Amanda Dobbs)

Yet, the formation of negative associations can be easily avoided if puppies are introduced to the veterinary environment in a positive fashion. Some clinics help with this by hosting puppy parties. This is where groups of puppies and their owners are invited, outside normal hours, to meet the staff, play with other puppies and interact with new people. When managed properly this not only creates positive associations with the practice, it also aids their general socialization.

Once fears have been established it can be difficult to overcome them and many dogs go through their entire lives being frightened of going to the vets. This could be considered a welfare issue, especially for dogs that require regular treatment or hospitalization. Whilst there are some useful prescription medications that can be used to alleviate a dog's distress, a programme of desensitization and counter-conditioning treatment can help. We will be returning to these treatment strategies later in the book.

Generalized Anxiety Disorder

A dog that has generalized anxiety is one that is constantly on high alert. They may be susceptible to at least one of, or a combination of, the aforementioned fear-related problems and therefore represent a significant welfare concern. These dogs invariably require professional input from a veterinary surgeon who can prescribe suitable medication to be given alongside a behaviour modification plan.

Effects of Chronic Stress on Mental and Physical Health

Long-term exposure to stressful situations is detrimental to mental and physical health and for that reason problems should be addressed without delay. Stress affects dogs of all ages but, in puppies and young dogs, it can interfere with their physical growth and can compromise brain development. If left to continue, the ongoing effect of cortisol supresses the immune system leaving the dog susceptible to infections and medical problems. Impaired blood flow to the gastro-intestinal system causes digestive upsets and this in itself can heighten anxiety. Feeling stressed is also likely to cause muscle tension which affects normal movement. The fall-out being a greater risk of musculoskeletal injures or the aggravation of existing conditions.

Being in a state of high alert is mentally and physically draining too, and accordingly dogs are unable to relax which can lead to sleep deprivation. Although research is limited in dogs, anecdotal evidence suggests that, like humans, lack of good-quality sleep increases irritability, disturbs concentration and affects memory retention.

Key Take Home Points

- Fear, anxiety and phobia have different meanings but share similar emotional processes.
- The stress response is automatic and the dog has no control over the effects.
- The amygdala and hippocampus both play a vital role in controlling emotional behaviour and store memories of traumatic experiences.
- One single frightening event can be enough to set up a life-long, fear-related behaviour problem.
- Providing a dog with access to their coping strategies and giving them a sense of control and choice improves their ability to deal with stressful situations.
- Chronic stress is damaging to physical and mental health.
- Events that are novel, unpredictable and out of the dog's control are likely to cause stress.

CHAPTER 2

Factors that Influence the Level and Nature of Canine Fear and Anxiety

How a dog responds to and deals with a stressful situation varies considerably from one individual to another. Like humans, some dogs are more prone to anxiety than others and consequently find it harder to cope with stressors than more confident characters. Some develop chronic fear-related problems whereas others can recover from a traumatic experience without any long-term effects. So what is it that brings about this disparity between dogs? Answering that question isn't always easy because there are so many factors but essentially, it's down to the interplay between genetics, the environment and the influence of learning.

Genetics and Breeding

Genes are the basic units of heredity, made up of molecules called deoxyribonucleic acid, more commonly known as DNA. These molecules are the blueprint of an individual, carrying all the coding responsible for how they function, their temperament and physical attributes. Genes are passed from each parent to their offspring throughout the generations so how a dog behaves and deals with stress is strongly affected by their genetic make-up.

Genetic research in dogs has already identified specific genes responsible for anxiety and some breeds have been shown to have a greater prevalence for certain fear-related problems, suggesting a genetic component. For example, Border Collies and other related herding breeds have been identified as having a higher propensity for fear of noises. Of course this doesn't mean that all of this breed type will be affected but knowing about their susceptibility can be useful, especially when planning their habituation and socialization to noises.

Variance of breed can also affect the way a dog expresses its fear and this is most likely related to what a dog was actually selectively bred to do. For example, the terrier group of dogs has a long history of being bred to hunt both above and below ground. Being sent down a dark hole to flush out foxes, rats and other quarry requires a confident, bold temperament. Consequently, these breeds are more likely to have a genetic predisposition to display what appear to be confident responses to fear such as barking and running towards the threat. Conversely, breeds like the Cavalier King Charles Spaniel, known for being a gentle companion dog, may choose a less robust response and instead use avoidance and more appeasing styles of behaviour. However, this doesn't indicate that one dog is feeling more or less frightened than another – they are just expressing it differently.

OPPOSITE: Puppies, courtesy of Rebecca Wilkinson, Operation K9 Hydrotherapy.

Terriers were bred for hunting and this is generally reflected in their behaviour. (Photo: Peggy, courtesy of Caroline O'Neill)

Temperament

Temperament refers to the biogenetically determined behavioural characteristics and tendencies that a dog is born with and is relatively stable and consistent throughout life. Temperament is sometimes measured on a shy-bold scale and, unsurprisingly, puppies bred from parents who are shy and timid are more likely to inherit fearful and anxious traits than those bred from bold and confident ones. Selective breeding is a sensible approach to reducing the risk. Proof of this has been shown in the breeding programme for the UK-based Guide Dogs for the Blind charity, which has been extremely effective in breeding against fear-associated behaviours.

Accordingly, conscientious breeders should select healthy, confident and stable parents to breed from and behavioural health should be high on their agenda. As

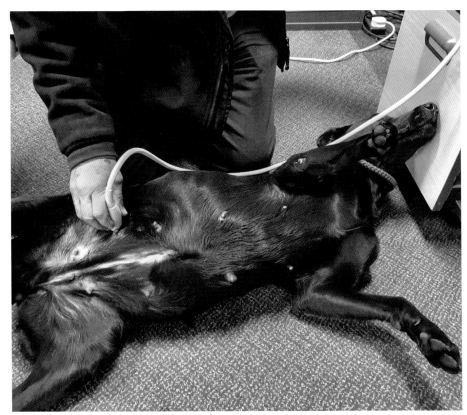

An ultrasound scan can help to diagnose pregnancy. Once confirmed, to safeguard the mother and her developing puppies, it is important to make sure she stays calm and free from stress. (Photo: Wren, courtesy of Rebecca Wilkinson, Operation K9 Hydrotherapy)

a precaution, I always advise anyone buying a puppy to insist on seeing the mother with the litter. If she appears fearful, nervous and reluctant to meet them in a friendly manner, then it's highly probable that these traits will be passed on to her offspring. Let's not forget that the sire (father) is responsible for fifty per cent of the genes too, so his behaviour is also relevant.

Epigenetics

Emerging from the field of genetics is a relatively new branch of research called epigenetics. Through this, we now know that maternal stress during pregnancy can also change the way genes are expressed in the developing foetus and that this can affect their post-natal development and behaviour. Although studies in dogs are limited, work done in humans and other animals shows raised levels of stress hormones in the mother can cross the placenta and modify her offspring's DNA profile. This can have an effect on the way their stress management systems develop rendering them more likely to be anxious, reactive individuals. Therefore, keeping the

mother calm and free from stressful encounters during her pregnancy could safeguard her and her puppies.

Another example of how a parent's experiences and environment can affect an animal's response to stressors later in life was demonstrated in a study of male and female mice, who were exposed to a specific scent during a fearful event. When this same scent was presented to their offspring, several generations down, astonishingly, it provoked a fear response (Dias and Ressler, 2014). Having an in-built alarm for anything deemed dangerous makes sense in evolutionary terms but what this study demonstrates is that adversity can have a long-term effect, not just on the individual, but also on their successive progeny.

Maternal Styles and Social Learning

Turning to the environment, the nature of maternal care in the post-natal period can affect a puppy's behavioural

Physical contact with an attentive mother makes it more likely that puppies will develop into emotionally stable adults. (Photo: Tweed, courtesy of Rebecca Wilkinson, Operation K9 Hydrotherapy)

development and good-quality mothering has been shown to increase social engagement and help proof against stress. Like most species, puppies need to be nurtured once they are born and so the amount of nuzzling, licking and attentiveness in the first few weeks of life are important. Hand-reared and orphaned puppies have a greater likelihood of developing problems associated with anxiety later in life, which supports the significance of the dam's early influence on the behaviour of her offspring. Early adoption (prior to eight weeks of age) has been shown to affect behavioural development leading to excessive barking, fearfulness on walks, attention-seeking behaviours and reactivity to noises.

Puppies also pay close attention to how their mother interacts socially and how she responds and reacts to a given situation. These observations are designed to help an animal learn what things might be considered dangerous and how to behave with others, a phenomenon called social learning. To help illustrate the point, it might be useful to think about our own species. Children whose parents show a dislike towards a particular food or who are frightened of spiders tend to adopt the same dislikes and fears. In the same way, if a puppy sees its parents displaying fear-related behaviours and high reactivity towards certain stimuli, then they are likely to learn to respond in a similar fashion.

Although social learning is primarily learned from the mother, puppies (and even older dogs) can learn from their owners and other animals they are in contact with too. Consequently, if a puppy is housed with another dog that has a fear of strangers or if the owner startles whenever they experience a thunderstorm, they will be teaching the puppy that these things represent danger, which can affect the way they respond and can set them up for problems later in life.

Social learning isn't just between the mother and her offspring. Important lessons can also be learned from older dogs with whom a puppy resides. (Photo: Myrtle and Zara, courtesy of Amanda Dobbs)

Canine Behavioural Development and Early Learning

Once puppies are born, work can begin on preparing them for life's stressors and this can be done through the process of habituation. This involves introducing (habituating) puppies regularly and sensitively to a raft of everyday things so that they gradually become used to them. Being kept in isolation would cause them to be startled by the simplest of things such as the sound of a washing machine, dishwasher, vacuum cleaner and other everyday stimuli. Therefore, the sooner this process can begin the better.

The Neonatal Period (Up to two weeks of age)

Habituation involves all the senses and it's during the neonatal period that the first ones, which are touch and smell, develop. In this period, puppies can be introduced

to the scent of people and other animals. Although this may occur naturally, articles of clothing or scent cloths can be used to harvest and transfer scents from various sources.

Preparing Scent Cloths

- Prepare several small, clean cotton cloths, about the size of a small handkerchief.
- Eradicate existing scents by pre-boiling and air-drying before use.
- Scents from other household pets (such as cats, rabbits) can be harvested by stroking them gently with the cloth and then introducing these in to the whelping box.
- Do not use the scent from unvaccinated dogs and be mindful of the transfer of infection.

Early exposure to safe handling helps to habituate a puppy to being touched by humans. (Photo: George with Dachshund puppy, courtesy of Lindsey Westwood, Hopewood Dachshunds)

Gentle handling and stroking the pup (known as gentling) should also begin and continue throughout the socialization period as this helps puppies get used to being handled and prevents fearfulness towards people later in life. A scientific study of puppies that had undergone deliberate gentling between day three and day twenty-one showed that they spent more time exploring, coped better with isolation and were calmer at eight weeks of age when compared to puppies who hadn't undergone the same procedure (Gazzano *et al.*, 2008).

The Transitional Period (From two to three weeks of age)

During this period a puppy's eyes and ears open, so habituating them to sounds and sights should begin now. They start to move around (albeit a bit wobbly to begin with) and social and exploratory behaviours begin. Moving the whelping box to a safe place in the home where there are more comings and goings can help expose them to the everyday sounds, sights and smells of a household.

Although it's important to include a wide range of stimuli, care should be taken not to bombard or overwhelm them. For example, extremely loud noises could cause the development of noise sensitivities and sensitize (the opposite to habituation) the puppy to stimuli, which is obviously counter-productive. Habituation should

Interactions with a docile adult dog can be a beneficial experience for young puppies. (Photo: Brie, courtesy of Rebecca Wilkinson)

continue and run alongside the next important phase of a puppy's development.

The Socialization Period (From three to twelve to fourteen weeks of age)

The sensitive period for canine socialization begins at around three weeks and lasts until they are around twelve to fourteen weeks old. This is a critical period because it is when puppies are extremely sensitive to learning. Their brains are rapidly developing and all their senses are functional so they begin to take in everything going on around them, both good and bad. A concerted effort should be made to teach puppies life-skills now and, because the timeframe for this is relatively narrow, it's crucial that there isn't a delay.

It's during this time when they are most influenced by social experiences so it is important to give them positive and sensitive exposure to a wide variety of things, situations and people that they are likely to encounter throughout life. Social interactions with their mother, littermates and their human carers will begin the process but they need to widen this experience as soon as they can and, unless the breeder is putting them through a programme of socialization themselves, there are implications for puppies who stay with the breeder for most, or all, of their socialization period. Once they are beyond fourteen weeks of age it becomes virtually impossible to catch up

and the puppies will be fearful in almost all new situations. A carefully planned behaviour modification plan will help but it's unlikely that they will ever be 'normal' and they will require lifelong behaviour management.

Key to the success of socialization is the way it is done. The most important thing to remember is to make sure the puppy isn't overwhelmed or traumatized. Throwing them in the deep end is a recipe for disaster and can cause more harm than good.

Weaning begins during the socialization period (at around four weeks of age), so it's a good time to briefly introduce the role that good nutrition plays in behavioural development. In the first few months of life a puppy's brain grows rapidly and good nutrition will support its development. Learning depends on good brain function and socialization is all about learning. Consequently, early nutrient deficiencies can stunt long-term brain function and impair cognition, which impacts on behaviour throughout life.

The benefits of proper socialization cannot be over-emphasized. Without it a puppy is more likely to be timid, show fear and high reactivity towards other dogs and people and go on to develop problematic fear-related behaviours in the future. Positive experiences encountered in the socialization period can diminish if not repeated, so appropriate interactions with people and other animals should continue until after the adolescent

Interacting and engaging with friendly dogs teaches puppies some important key life skills. (Photo: Nugget and Bramble, courtesy of Helen Milner)

Puppies should be introduced to less common sights and sounds to ensure they have a well-rounded socialization experience. (Photo: Teddy, courtesy of Jordan Lapping)

period which, depending on the individual, can be up to twenty-four months of age.

Sensitive Fear Periods

During a puppy's development there are times when they are more sensitive to frightening situations, and these are called fear periods. The first fear period occurs during the socialization phase, somewhere around seven to ten weeks of age but this varies considerably. For example, a study by Mary Morrow and her colleagues showed that the onset of fear-related avoidance behaviour was much earlier in German Shepherds (before six weeks of age) than some other breeds. Knowing this means that extra care can be taken when planning their socialization.

Unfortunately, the first fear period usually coincides with the time the puppy leaves the mother as well as their first trip to the veterinary clinic for their vaccinations. A sensitive transition from the breeder to the new home and a positive vaccination experience at the vets are therefore of prime importance.

The second fear period kicks in anywhere from around six months of age when the dog begins to reach puberty.

This is the time when a dog becomes sexually mature and dramatic hormonal changes can make a young dog more sensitive and react in a highly emotional fashion, just like us! Again, a sensitive approach is required to help a dog through this time and being sensitive to their training needs is important.

Adolescence

From puberty the dog enters the adolescent phase, which typically lasts until eighteen months of age but can be up to two years. As well as hormonal activity, the juvenile brain undergoes changes as it adapts and remodels itself into an adult brain. Behavioural effects can include a reduced ability to control their impulses and emotions, increased irritability, showing fear of things that haven't bothered them in the past and disobedience. It is important to be mindful of the behavioural changes that can arise during adolescence and other sensitive periods because a bad experience may have a lasting effect. Socialization techniques should be revisited and sensitive management is called for otherwise fear-related behavioural problems can develop which can have long-term consequences.

The onset of the first sensitive fear period is earlier in the German Shepherd than some other breeds. (Photo: Nala, courtesy of Michael Rowland)

A young dog can be emotionally vulnerable around puberty and adolescence, so a careful and sensitive approach is necessary. (Photo: Jessie, courtesy of Amy Crossley)

Canine Post-Traumatic Stress Disorder

It is now believed that traumatic experiences can lead to post-traumatic stress disorder (PTSD), similar to that seen in humans. Although research is limited in dogs, much can be gleaned by drawing on studies conducted in humans and useful parallels help to make a diagnosis.

Canine PTSD is suspected after a dog has experienced a real, or perceived, traumatic event and then goes on to develop persistent generalized behavioural problems that were not present before the trauma. Examples of the types of traumas that have been associated with PTSD include being involved in a fire or explosion, experiencing traumatic injuries, being attacked by another dog, severe physical abuse or abandonment and long-term hospitalization in the veterinary clinic.

Symptoms vary but include generalized anxiety, the development of fear and fear-aggression, hypervigilance, avoidance, withdrawal, separation-related disorders and sleep disturbances.

Negative Association Learning

No dog, even those with emotionally stable parents, an attentive dam and a good habituation and socialization experience, is immune to the things that life throws at them and, unfortunately, sometimes bad experiences happen. While it is true that dogs with a better start in life have more resilience, sometimes, after a dog has experienced trauma, they remain on guard and feel perpetually afraid that something bad is going to happen again. At other times the negative experiences are associated with things that were going on at the same time. For example, a dog handled roughly by a child may go on to develop a fear of children or a dog that suffers from travel sickness may gain a fear of being in the car. This is called negative association learning and can explain how and why fears develop. We shall be concentrating on the impact of learning later in the book but suffice to say these types of life experience can have a profound impact on a dog's level of fear and anxiety.

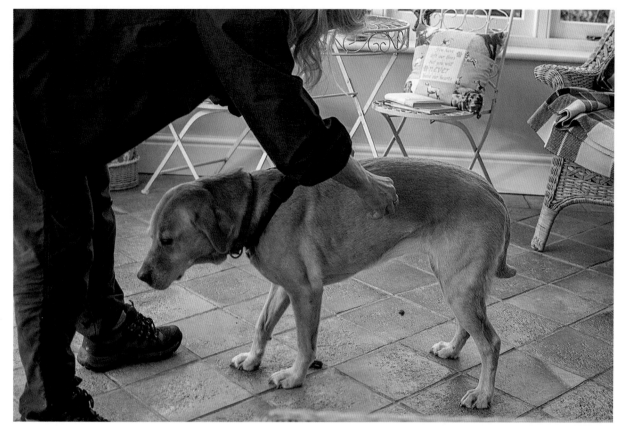

Approaching and handling a dog without due care and attention can be the cause of anxiety. Notice the subtle signs of stress, for example a lowered posture and changes in the expressions. (Photo: Millie and Caroline)

Human Interaction

The way we interact and socialize with a dog can contribute to their level of fear and anxiety. Even routine interactions can be a cause of concern for them and it's these exchanges that are more likely to go unnoticed. For example, leaning over them to get harnesses and leads attached in preparation for taking them out can often provoke low-level stress signals, so look out for the tell-tale signs.

An inconsistent approach, confrontational training styles and the use of punishment are high on the list of stressors. Punishers can include shouting, rattling a can of stones or more punitive methods such as the use of shock and pinch collars, jerking on a lead or hitting and smacking a dog.

It is not surprising that the risk of developing or heightening fear-related behaviours increases if punishment and aversive training methods are used. Studies have found that they lead to a greater frequency of aggression and excitability and the chance of aggression towards family members and unfamiliar people is also increased. Moreover, a study designed to evaluate the effects of training methods on dog welfare showed that a higher frequency of punishment was correlated with higher anxiety and fear scores (Vieira de Castro *et al.*, 2020).

Unfortunately, some people still believe in the 'Dominance Theory', that dogs should be trained using dominance and force. This style of training is based on the myth that dogs are like wolves and, in order to gain control, are motivated to achieve a higher social status relative to others in the pack. As a consequence, some owners and trainers still use techniques that are based on dominating dogs to make them more biddable. 'Showing the dog who is the boss' is a common mantra and staring them out, pinning them down and performing alpha rolls are still practised. Yet, recent observations of wolf society have taught us that they have a far more harmonious relationship than first purported and we now know that the domestic dog has its own evolutionary niche, far removed from that of wolves. Therefore, we can safely conclude that using these methods is outmoded and that they are likely to lead to fear, anxiety and aggression as well as damage the human-dog relationship.

Another fall-out from using confrontation and aversive styles of training is something called learned helplessness. This occurs when a dog has come to expect pain, suffering, or emotional discomfort without any means of escape. As a result of not knowing what they need to do – they just shut down completely and stop trying.

Pain and its Role in Behaviour

Pain can lead to generalized anxiety and self-defensive behaviours and can lower the threshold for fear, reactivity and aggression. The behavioural signs of pain include:

- Any of the stress signals
- Aggression and reactivity
- Irritability
- Withdrawal
- Lethargy
- Vocalization (for example groaning, yelping)
- Pacing (due to anxiety and discomfort)

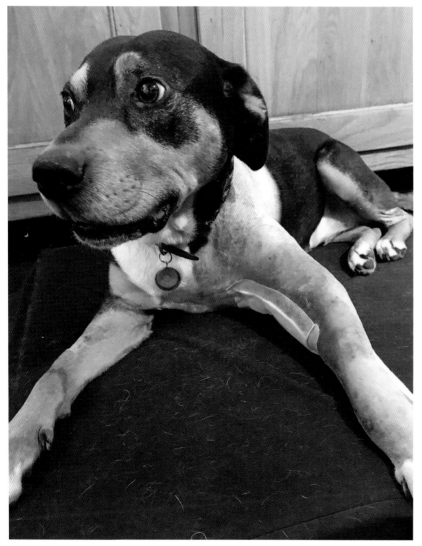

Pain and discomfort can lower the threshold for fear and anxiety. Notice the facial tension and dilated pupils. (Photo: Elvis, courtesy of Sophie White)

Some of the sources of pain and discomfort that have been more commonly linked to stress and fear-related behaviours include musculoskeletal pain, particularly arthritic joints, skin disorders (which can be irritating and itchy) and gastro-intestinal pain.

It is widely accepted that in humans, stress and anxiety leads to indigestion, irritable bowels and an altogether unpleasant feeling in our stomachs. It shouldn't be too difficult therefore for us to appreciate that dogs can be affected in similar ways. The term 'gut-brain axis' refers to the constant bidirectional communication between the gastro-intestinal (GI) tract and the brain. This is done through a network of hundreds of millions of neurons collectively called the enteric nervous system, sometimes referred to as the 'second brain'. Put simply, being anxious can lead to gut problems and gut problems can lead to anxiety. Before long a vicious cycle of events can be triggered and this affects the dog's well-being.

There are times when pain and discomfort go undiagnosed. This isn't a criticism of the vet's know-how but, when it comes to dealing with pain, dogs tend to conceal it. This is especially so when they are in an environment that is less familiar or where they feel threatened. Also at the veterinary clinic they are often tense which makes examination much more difficult and sometimes symptoms are not obvious. Getting a dog examined by a

> ### How to Rule Out Painful Conditions
>
> - Rule out pain by getting a veterinary examination (even if there are no obvious signs of pain or illness).
> - Speak to the veterinary surgeon about investigations that may help with diagnosis (such as diagnostic scans, blood sampling and X-rays).
> - Some vets may consider trialling analgesics (pain-killers). If they help it may suggest pain is present.
> - Take video recordings and pictures so that you, the veterinary surgeon and a behaviourist can look for subtle signs of pain.

veterinary surgeon is still important as further tests may reveal something that is being masked.

The way medical issues can be linked with behaviour problems was illustrated in a review of cases seen by animal behaviour clinicians at Lincoln University. They estimated that around a third of referred behaviour cases involved some form of painful condition and that

Sensory deficits and cognitive changes can lead to increased anxiety in the older dog. (Photo: Solo, courtesy of Rachael Egan)

fearful dogs that startled easily were possibly, in part, also responding to undiagnosed pain in their muscles or joints. This could lead to an association with the pain and the frightening stimulus, adding yet another aversive dimension to the problem. However, more encouragingly, the study did state that when pain was identified and treated, the problem behaviour was likely to improve.

Ageing

So far, I have concentrated on the factors that influence young dogs but at the other end of the spectrum is the elderly (geriatric) dog and they should not be forgotten. As dogs age there is a tendency for them to become affected by hearing and sight loss and, although they cope with a gradual decline, sudden onset loss or impairment can cause heightened fear and anxiety. It's important to remember that deaf dogs sleep very deeply, so they should always be woken gently to avoid startling them. Also, partial deafness may hinder a dog's ability to locate the sound of a fearful stimulus which can be confusing and frightening. Blind and deaf dogs may also develop separation problems because they are unable to know when an owner has left them and suddenly feel alone and isolated when they realize they are not around.

Fear-related problems that emerge with age can also be associated with canine cognitive dysfunction (CCD), a process that affects geriatric dogs in a similar way to that of humans with dementia. Symptoms of disorientation and loss of memory can affect the dog's ability to locate familiar resources and locations, all of which may well be a source of anxiety. Because age-related diseases and organ failure may also be involved, it is especially important that a full clinical examination is performed by the veterinary surgeon.

Key Take Home Points

- Genetics, the environment and learning are intertwined and together can influence the level and expression of canine fear and anxiety.
- In-utero and other early life stressors can lead to the development of fear-related problems in adulthood.
- Epigenetics gives us a new outlook on the origins and early development of fear.
- Puppies require positive and appropriate habituation and socialization learning experiences in order to become emotionally stable individuals.
- Negative association learning and aversive training methods can be responsible for, and exacerbate, fear, anxiety and aggression.
- Pain is linked with fear and anxiety.
- Geriatric dogs with cognitive and sensory impairments are susceptible to developing fear-related problems.

CHAPTER 3

Canine Communication: Decoding and Recognizing the Signs of Fear and Anxiety

Dogs are a social species, equipped with a rich repertoire of behaviours and body postures. These are necessary to convey messages to others in the group enabling them to express emotions, avoid conflict and gain resources and desired outcomes. Because the dog has a unique evolutionary history with humans, these same signals are very often directed towards us. Communication towards a different species is called interspecific communication and, for the most part, we can understand what they mean. For example, most dog owners recognize when their dog is feeling content and relaxed as opposed to showing obvious signs of fear, such as cowering and hiding. Nevertheless, some of the more subtle signs can be missed, particularly those that indicate when they are unsure, concerned or mildly stressed.

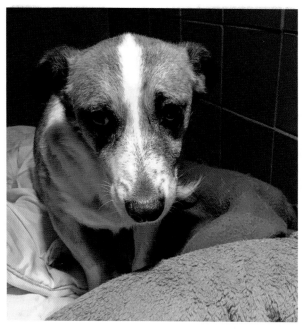

A dog in a relaxed pose, which most owners are able to identify. (Photo: Millie)

A dog showing signs of distress, which can sometimes be missed by owners. (Photo: Shelly, courtesy of Holly Barker)

OPPOSITE: Darcy and Jem, courtesy of Karyn Harper and Lora Lane.

Learning to decode canine communication signals is extremely useful when it comes to helping or working with nervous dogs. Firstly, because it informs us how they are feeling and secondly, it prompts us to respond in a way that helps them out of a frightening situation before things escalate. Demonstrating our understanding opens up the line of communication, promoting trust and giving the dog a greater sense of security when they are with us.

Methods of Communication

Olfactory Communication (Scent and Smell)

One extremely well-developed sense by which dogs communicate and understand the world around them is through smell. The dog has around 250 million or so olfactory receptors in their brain. When you compare that to the five million or so in humans it gives you some idea of the part that smell plays in their lives and the way they use it to gather information. This highly refined sense can detect an odour diluted at one to two parts per trillion. To put that in to some sort of perspective, Dr Alexander Horowitz, a professor of canine cognition at Barnard College in New York, has compared it to them being able to detect a teaspoon of sugar in a million gallons of water – that's two Olympic-sized swimming pools full!

Messages conveyed through scent can be either direct communication, when two individuals meet, or through indirect communication via scent marking. Dogs do this by depositing their scent in urine, faeces, anal sac secretions and body odours. Within these deposits are chemical molecules (chemo-signals), which play a large role in the transmission of information about things such as health, reproductive status and emotional state.

Most interactions between dogs involve olfactory investigation and, when left to their own devices, a great deal of sniffing takes place. Initially this is concentrated in areas where the scent-producing glands are most dense, around the face, neck and anal region. This greeting ritual is where the exchange of information takes place and social assessments are made. Some less well-socialized dogs are not equipped to understand this social etiquette and just wade in, which can be a source of tension and conflict.

Pheromones

Chemo-signals are also contained in something called pheromones. Pheromones are scents that are not necessarily detected at a conscious level but, when sensed by an animal of the same species, they trigger a specific reaction. For example, fear pheromones from anal gland secretions are expelled in extreme fear and alarm and they alert and warn others to danger. It is very likely that it's these pheromones that dogs pick up on when they walk in to the veterinary clinic and helps explain why some dogs who have never been there before can show fearful responses.

Anal glands are situated on either side of the opening of the anus, producing a semi-viscous fluid that is emptied during defaecation. To the human nose, anal gland

Dogs can glean detailed information about one another by sniffing areas where there is an abundance of scent producing glands. (Photo: Jem and Maisie, courtesy of Karyn Harper and Tracy Chapman)

Dogs can detect and interpret information from the chemical molecules contained in deposits left behind by other dogs. (Photo: Millie, courtesy of Tommy Taylor)

Sniffing around the anus is part of a dog's normal greeting behaviour and pheromones and unique scents provide an exchange of information. (Photo: Maisie and Woody, courtesy of Tracy Chapman and Mo Lake)

secretions smell fishy and unpleasant but the odour is actually unique to each dog and is a means of identifying themselves to others as well as providing information about their emotional state.

Some scents and pheromones can induce calmness and thereby modify behaviour. For example, when bitches are rearing puppies, they produce a pheromone from the area around the mammary glands called the dog appeasing pheromone (DAP). This scent is believed to have a calming effect on puppies during suckling and is perhaps one of the reasons why they appear content when close to the mother.

Does our scent affect dogs behaviourally?

Stories of dogs being able to smell our fear have been perpetuated for many years and it turns out that this may be true. One particular study tested whether dogs could detect human emotions by showing a group of people films that were designed to cause fear, happiness or a neutral response. Afterwards, samples of their sweat were collected and presented to the dogs during which time their behaviours and heart rates were monitored. The results were revealing. Dogs who were given the scent of people who were frightened showed more signs of stress than those dogs who were exposed to happy or neutral smells. They also had higher heart rates, sought more reassurance from their owners and made less social contact with strangers (D'Aniello *et al.*, 2018).

Dogs also seem to be attuned to familiar human odours. Indeed, in the veterinary context it is common practice to ask an owner to bring a piece of their clothing

The dog appeasing pheromone, emitted from around the mother's mammary glands, has a calming influence on the suckling puppy. (Photo: Puppy, courtesy of Lindsey Westwood, Hopewood Dachshunds)

along to help provide comfort and reassurance for their hospitalized dog. We now have proof that this really can help through using magnetic resonance imaging (MRI) which has shown familiar human scents activate parts of the brain associated with positive expectations and social reward.

Auditory Communication (Vocalization and Hearing)

Dogs communicate with one another by using a range of different sounds (Table 3.1). They can glean a lot of information just from these sounds alone and, a bit like us, are able to discriminate between agonistic and non-threatening vocalizations without being able to see each other. Dogs are very effective at using vocalizations to communicate with humans too and tapping into their vocal repertoire can help us determine the emotional content and gain a better idea about how they are feeling.

Barking is a way that most dogs communicate. (Photo: Millie)

Barking and growling

The bark usually alters in pitch and tone depending on the meaning. For example, higher pitched barks interspersed with whines generally denote calls for attention, distress or sometimes just general excitement during greetings. Conversely, lower pitched barks and growls are largely used to issue a warning. Frank, forthright aggression however is usually quiet.

Barking behaviour can be used as a group activity too and sometimes is a call to arms. This behaviour is often evident in multi-dog households, when someone comes to the door. When one barks – they all join in and mirror and stimulate one another. If we shout to quieten them it's possible they think we are joining in too, which is probably why it rarely helps!

Growls are usually used in close distance communication. Humans have been programmed to view the dog growl as unacceptable and an aggressive behaviour that should be punished. However, whilst it makes sense to heed it as a warning, growling is actually a clear signal and one that we should listen and respond to. If not, there is a danger that the dog will stop conversing, suppress the growl and take more decisive action leading to a snap or a bite. Therefore, the best way to deal with a growling dog is to help it feel less threatened by backing off or remove it from the thing that they are growling at. Follow this up by analysing why the dog was growling in the first place and see if you can learn anything from your reflections. In many cases their motivation is based on fear.

Hearing

The dog has a superior sense of hearing to ours so they can hear things before us. This is worth noting when using recordings of sounds as part of a desensitization treatment protocol for a noise-sensitive dog. What sounds very quiet to us may not be for the dog. Playing recordings too loudly is one reason why this technique can fail.

Growling and snarling can be used as a warning, as seen here in a dog guarding her food bowl. (Photo: Jessie, courtesy of Amy Crossley)

Table 3.1. Examples of canine vocalizations that can (along with other behavioural signs) indicate fear and anxiety.

Auditory Communication	Message	Comments
Crying/whimper/whine	• Appeasement • Distress • Defence • Pain • Greeting • Attention-seeking	Whining is one of the first noises a puppy makes.
Growl/snarl	• Defence • Warning • Agonistic	Not to be confused with play growling.
Bark	• Alarm • Defence • Calling for attention • Warning • Excitement	Changes in tone, increased frequency or when used as a first response to hearing sudden noises or seeing strangers are indications of fear and anxiety.
Howl	• Calling for attention • Announcing presence	Often emitted when the dog is separated from the attachment figure as in separation-related problems. Siberian Huskies and Malamutes will often howl together as part of their normal, breed-specific behaviour.
Yelp	• Withdrawal • To gain a response	The context of the situation needs to be taken in to account.

Source: Adapted from Bowen and Heath (2005).

A dog's superior sense of hearing helps them to pick up vocalizations from other dogs some distance away. (Photo: Jenga, courtesy of Jemma Whitford, Ruffmuts Training and Behaviour)

The dog's hearing is more sensitive to higher frequency sounds than ours. This means that they can be adversely affected by certain sound frequencies that don't bother us, some of which can be found in most homes. To determine the effects of household noises on canine stress levels researchers at the University of California revealed that the most intense signs of fear were observed when dogs heard sudden, intermittent high-frequency noises, particularly the bleeps emitted from low battery warnings on smoke detectors and their alarms. It was proposed that these noises could even cause pain to their ears, posing a welfare issue. Most concerning was that a high proportion of the owners in the study were unaware of the signs of stress or found their dogs' reactions a source of amusement.

Other devices that operate on high frequency sound waves include ultrasonic pest deterrents. These are not detected by most human ears although some younger adults can hear them and have reported that they cannot endure them for very long. As the study points out, each dog copes with stressors in different ways and so

Head tilts can help capture sound but it is more commonly seen when a dog is engaging with an owner. (Photo: Rollie, courtesy of Amy Crossley)

some dogs may not display obvious signs of stress. But this doesn't mean they are not affected by them. The best line of action is to conduct a noise audit in your home, change batteries regularly and avoid exposing dogs to ultrasonic devices.

When compared to humans, a dog's ability to detect where a sound is coming from is poor. We believe that this might be a contributing factor for sound-sensitive dogs during thunderstorms or fireworks – they are not sure where the scary thing is coming from!

With age, a dog's hearing can decline and this is sometimes another reason for elderly dogs developing fearful behaviours and startling when approached, especially if they are asleep. Blowing a soft, gentle, breath of air onto their fur to waken them is a method I find useful.

Tactile Communication (Touch)

The sense of touch is another important means of canine communication. Closely bonded dogs will lie close together when resting and there is a great deal of contact during play and other affiliative behaviours. Dogs will often seek close contact with owners too and jump up at them, lie at their feet or lean against them to maintain close proximity, especially in times of emotional discomfort.

Other forms of contact can be less positive. A dog issuing a threat to another will sometimes place its head over their victim's back, forming a T shape. In this way they manipulate their movements and exert control. As humans, we need to be mindful of this during handling and restraint as it is possible to almost recreate this action and inadvertently convey the wrong message, causing a dog to feel uncomfortable and fearful. This is particularly the case when examining a dog in a veterinary context or during grooming.

Stroking and petting a dog is our way of showing affection towards them but not all dogs find it relaxing. In fact, if you look closely, some dogs show mild anxiety and withdraw when being touched on certain parts of the body such as the top of the head and paws, even by people who are well-known to them. In general dogs seem to favour being stroked under the chin, on the shoulders or on the chest, between their front legs. It is also possible to transfer our anxiety and cause a dog to become alert and less relaxed by the way we stroke and pet them. Rapid, quick, short stroking, especially around the head and face, is less likely to induce calmness than longer and slower stroking. Dogs that are keen to be touched will often lean in to you or nudge you to continue.

The way children interact with dogs can be a source of stress. Wrapping arms around their necks, staring, leaning and looming over whilst cuddling them can be misinterpreted as a threat and may result in the dog using some form of aggression to try and repel them. Unfortunately, the dog is very often blamed for their lack of tolerance and chastised, rehomed or, in the worst case scenario, put to sleep. Educating families and children is key.

What Dogs See

Before moving on to how dogs gather and convey information from seeing one another's body language, it helps to have some idea about their eyesight. The typical dog has 20/75 visual acuity in comparison to our 20/20 vision. This means that what a person with normal eyesight can see at 23m (75ft) away, a dog would only see at 6m (20ft) away, so surprisingly, it's much less keen than ours. In terms of colour it is believed that dogs can't discern the differences between green, yellow, and red colours, almost like humans with colour blindness but how this affects a dog behaviourally is still not certain.

Dogs are adapted to see in dim light and are more sensitive to bright lights, which means it can take longer for their eyes to adapt when moving from bright lights to darker conditions. It is therefore possible that an abrupt change of light that impairs their vision could be a source of stress for some dogs. Something worth considering, particularly if a frightened dog was moved from, let's say, a brightly lit consulting room at a veterinary clinic into a hospital ward with dimmer lighting.

Assessing and Interpreting Body Language

The dog has an extensive range of signalling and, provided they have been well socialized, are masters at deciphering subtle gestures and postures between one another. However, they use this skill extremely well to interpret our body postures too and generally can read us better than we can read them. Yet, with practice and close observations we can also become much more proficient at this skill and learn to recognize the indicators of canine fear and anxiety with more ease.

Facial Expressions

As already seen, when a dog feels fearful and anxious, the face holds many clues. Facial muscles often become tense, the ear position can alter and the skin is tight. This is particularly evident around the jaw line with the commissures (corners of the mouth) being drawn back and tight.

The eyes have been described as windows to the soul and undoubtedly they can offer some insight into a dog's emotions. Depending on the context, when a dog feels under stress, the eyes can sometimes appear to squint or may be wide open with the pupils dilated (because of the influence of adrenaline). Fast rapid blinking is also a sign of stress whereas a slow blinking, soft, relaxed eye demonstrates contentment and relaxation.

A dog will often turn their head away and avert their eyes if they feel threatened or wish to avoid confrontation although, very often they will express their anxiety by showing part of the whites of the eyeball (the sclera) which appears as a white crescent in the bottom part of

Facial tension, rigid ears and wide, staring eyes communicate distress and fear in this dog. (Photo: Tilly, courtesy of Rob and Jane Sparkes)

Turning the head away and avoiding eye contact (the black dog) tells the other dog they do not wish to engage with them. (Photo: Molly and Milly, courtesy of Helen Molton)

45

Lip-licking and a 'whale eye' denotes stress. (Photo: Barney, courtesy of Allen Redfearn)

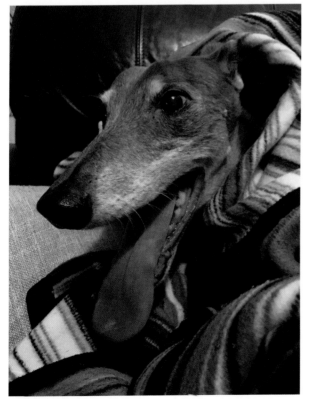

The commissures pulled back and a spatulate tongue signal distress in this dog. (Photo: Inka, courtesy of Jessica Prickett)

the eyeball often referred to as 'whale eye'. Conversely a hard stare is a threatening gesture, issued as a warning and often preceding a bite or attack.

The ear position can change dramatically when a dog is feeling insecure. Generally, a dog's ears are pulled back and close to their heads when they are feeling frightened or apprehensive or pricked and held more rigidly and erect when startled or listening out for something that is frightening. However, there is a great deal of breed variation and dogs that have floppy and less mobile ears, like Spaniels, tend to hold their ears closer to their face with the head in a lowered position, sometimes described as the 'hang-dog expression'.

Lip and nose licking, sometimes accompanied by jaw chomping, are common but subtle indicators of anxiety and distress. In more advanced levels of fear, salivation may be noted and panting can be observed due to the increase in their respiration rate. At the same time, the tongue can often be seen hanging from the mouth appearing rigid and spatula shaped. Yawning is another subtle signal, sometimes occurring after a fearful event and thought to denote stress relief. Yet, it can be detected in many other contexts where the dog feels emotionally uncomfortable and is one to look out for.

Pulling the lips back to reveal the teeth as if grinning is not, as is often misinterpreted, a smile or greeting gesture. Although it is often seen in that context, it is usually accompanied with a lower body stance and fast blinking or half-closed eyes, reflecting the dog's signal of non-threat and appeasement.

Body Postures and Movements

How a dog stands and postures can give us some useful information. A lower posture with the weight distributed on the hind quarters infers lack of confidence and cowering or a side-on stance, sometimes with a front paw raised, are non-threatening body postures that communicate that they are frightened and wish to avoid conflict. Similarly, exposing the underside of the body demonstrates vulnerability and low threat and may be accompanied with urination. But we must take care. A dog in any of these non-threatening poses can still use aggression if they feel threatened and can rapidly make the transition from freeze to flight to fight.

Slow movements with a low, almost crawl-like, carriage are sometimes exhibited when a dog expects some conflict, common when an owner is shouting angrily at their dog as it returns to them after it has run off (which, by the way, is one reason why some dogs don't come when called).

When the hairs along the back are raised (known as piloerection), it is often interpreted as a sign of aggression. However, this can also signal anxiety, fear or just general arousal. The likely function of piloerection is to try to look larger and more threatening to an opponent. The human equivalent is when someone stands taller or places their hands on their hips to appear more powerful and superior. On the outside they may look threatening but invariably, on the inside, they feel vulnerable.

Approaching and then quickly retreating from a frightening stimulus is another motor behaviour that dogs demonstrate when fearful. This is known as approach-avoidance conflict behaviour and occurs when an animal is drawn to investigate or approach something or somebody but at the same time is apprehensive about

advancing closer. Examples include when a dog hears something they want to explore or when being lured with food. Given that a dog in a fearful state it is more likely to startle and any sudden noise or movement may cause a rapid and violent fear-aggressive response, luring a dog towards us when they are frightened is inadvisable and potentially dangerous.

Curved body postures

When observing dogs meeting off-lead, it is rare to see them approach one another head-on. In fact, a major trigger for a dog that is fearful of strangers and other dogs is when they are being forced to walk directly towards them, especially when they are on a narrow pavement.

Given the choice, dogs tend to walk towards one another with a curved body posture. Therefore it makes sense to try and emulate the same method when walking a dog on a lead. Making minor changes to create space

The tail posture and stance of these two dogs shows which one feels the most confident in this interaction. (Photo: Maisie and Woody, courtesy of Tracy Chapman and Mo Lake)

and allowing them more freedom to do what comes naturally can help reduce anxiety and lessens the risk of them developing defensive aggression. We can even adopt a circuitous approach ourselves when we approach a dog, particularly one that we are unfamiliar with. This is piece of advice I pass on to veterinary personnel or anyone else who works with dogs and is particularly useful when approaching them in a kennel. Making a bee-line to get them out is a common trigger for fear and fear-aggression.

Tails

Depending on the breed, tails come in all sorts of shapes and sizes. For example traditional hunting breeds such as pointers have tails that are held horizontally in a straight line whereas Whippets and Greyhounds usually hold their tails between their hind legs. However, a dog's tail can reveal quite a lot about their emotional state. Typically, when they feel frightened, worried and stressed the tail is held low, clamped close to the anus, and sometimes tucked in between the hind legs.

One very common misconception is that a wagging tail indicates friendliness. In reality the speed and direction of the wag and the tail carriage are more indicative of how the dog is feeling. A relaxed and friendly dog usually has a tail wag that swishes loosely back and forth, sometimes in a circular motion with broad strokes. However, a tail suddenly raised in an upright posture with a high-speed, vibrating, wag may indicate that the dog is feeling aroused, alert or is about to run or attack. A low tail carriage with reluctant, possibly rapid wags and a lowered body posture can indicate fearfulness, apprehension and

Appeasement Signals

A number of fear-related body postures and gestures already mentioned are exhibited at times when a dog wishes to diffuse conflict, calm a situation or just to communicate that they do not wish to pose a threat. A kind of white flag or peace offering.

Collectively these gestures are known as appeasement signals although Turid Rugaas, a Norwegian behaviourist who has made extensive studies of canine body language, has called them 'calming signals'. These signs, although common in other scenarios, are typically observed when dogs approach one another and meet for the first time. In response, other well-socialized dogs tend to understand the signal and back off. We should do the same.

Signs to look out for include:

- Averting eyes
- 'Whale eye'
- Turning the head
- Side-on stance and leaning away
- Licking the lips and nose and chomping the jaw
- Grinning
- Yawning
- Curved body posture on initial meetings

'Whale eye' is an indicator of stress and can indicate a dog's discomfort with a situation. (Photo: Skylar, courtesy of Sharon Harris)

anxiety, particularly noticeable when the dog is being approached by a stranger.

Interestingly, dogs can convey and glean information from the direction of a tail wag. In one study it was found that dogs tended to wag their tails to the right when looking at something they wanted to approach but wagged their tails to the left when confronted with something they wanted to back away from. Also, when dogs were shown a silhouette of another dog wagging its tail to the right they were more relaxed but they exhibited signs of stress when seeing a dog wagging its tail to the left (Siniscalchi *et al.*, 2013).

It is also thought that tail posture and wagging distributes the dog's unique scent from the anal region. More confident dogs, who want to interact and be noticed or issue warnings, are more likely to have wagging and upright tails. Conversely, less confident and fearful dogs will want to avoid sharing their scent and go unnoticed. Therefore, they tend to adopt a lower tail carriage to cover the anal region, which masks their scent and presence.

Interpreting Stress Signals in Puppies and Young Dogs

Whilst the signs of fear and stress in puppies and young dogs mirror that of adult dogs it is not uncommon for them to use active submission. These behaviours are typically presented when the youngster is experiencing some emotional conflict, for example during veterinary examinations or when being groomed. Signs of active submission include:

- Fidgeting, rolling over and wriggling
- Jumping up
- Pawing
- Nuzzling
- Licking
- Other exuberant greeting or play routines

Dogs will avert the eyes and try to disengage if they feel uncomfortable, as demonstrated here by my prolonged eye contact. (Photo: Millie and Caroline)

It is surmised that these behaviours are a defensive strategy, demonstrating that they do not pose a threat. However, they may also serve to distract and divert the attention of others, which can relieve the pressure they feel under. Yet, these behaviours could be easily ignored or misinterpreted as confidence, over-exuberance or silly play behaviours. Instead of chastising them or ignoring the behaviour, these young dogs should be removed from a situation or supported by the owner or the caretaker. If not, fear-related behaviours may develop and, as the dog matures, they may begin to use more forceful, defensive fear behaviours.

Displacement Activities

During times of emotional conflict or social stress a dog may display a behaviour that seems completely out of context and totally displaced from the situation they are in. These are called displacement activities. Human equivalents are twiddling the thumbs, wringing the hands or biting the lips. Like us, many of these behaviours tend to be self-directed. Examples include: self-grooming, scratching themselves as if they were itchy or even chasing their tails. Shaking off, as if wet, is another displacement activity although, like a yawn, is often seen after a stressful incident. Sniffing the ground is another displacement signal that can be missed, mainly because this is a favourite occupation of most dogs. However it's a common one when dogs are outside their comfort zone and is therefore one to be aware of.

Making an Accurate Assessment

When assessing canine body language, rather than looking at just one signal in isolation, it's essential to make observations of whole body postures. Also, the situation and the environment that the dog is in should be taken into account. For example, when a dog is licking their nose and lips, chomping the jaw and salivating, is it because they are feeling anxious or is it because they have just eaten something extremely tasty? Or is a dog that's trembling and shaking, and holding its tail close to its anus, doing so because they are fearful or is it because it's a whippet, whose tail is conformed in this way and is excited in anticipation of chasing prey? We must look at the big picture to be sure our interpretation is correct.

Learning How to Respond to Signalling

Interpreting and understanding canine communication signals accurately can shape the way we interact with them. A slight dip in the body, lifting of a paw or a seemingly minor change in the ear position can give clues about how a dog is feeling. Being able to decipher their meanings prompts us to make minor adjustments so we don't pose a threat. For example, in our approach we can adopt a closed and lower body posture, avoiding direct eye contact and advancing circuitously and slowly.

Our response towards a dog's signalling makes a significant difference to the outcome too. Depending on the circumstances we can help them out in a number of ways; giving them space when they need it, allowing them to feel a sense of control (by leading them away from a frightening situation) or backing off in response to their signalling to give them time to process information. Responding in these ways not only diffuses a situation rapidly, it demonstrates to the dog that the message they are conveying has been understood, helping ease their anxiety.

Why Some Dogs Have Difficulties Understanding Each Other

Missed opportunities during the socialization period means that some puppies just never learn social skills. Hand-reared puppies are particularly disadvantaged because, having never mixed with their mother or littermates, they are not equipped with the ability to recognize or deal with social encounters. At other times owners can be over-zealous and interfere with normal canine interactions by picking their dogs up and preventing them from meeting, greeting and learning important life-skills. Conversely, some owners allow their dogs to be bad mannered and don't recognize when they need to intervene. Much like teaching a child to have good manners, we need to supervise and guide our dogs.

Another cause of social misunderstanding is perhaps due to the way humans have altered the dogs' physical appearance through selective breeding. Some breeds have an abundance of hair, which hides almost all facial features and makes piloerection impossible. Large floppy ears and truncated or docked tails can diminish important aspects of a dog's behavioural repertoire and brachycephalic-shaped skulls (in breeds such as Bulldogs and Pekinese) can interfere with facial expressions. As a consequence, some of these dogs cannot deliver important information and others find it hard to understand them leading to confusion, frustration and a level of anxiety on both sides.

Interpreting the facial signals of long-haired breeds can be difficult and may be a source of conflict between dogs. (Photo: Matisse, courtesy of Nikki Wilson)

Key Take Home Points

- Having an awareness of canine communication helps us to assess a dog's emotional state more accurately.
- Behaviour can change from moment to moment.
- We must read communication signals in the context of the situation and assess the dog as a whole.
- Responding to a dog's signalling can open up the lines of communication, enhance their sense of security and prevent an escalation of fear and aggression.

CHAPTER 4

Aggression, Frustration and Reactivity: Their Links with Fear and Anxiety

Aggression

If we are to fully understand aggression we must appreciate that aggressive behaviour is usually motivated by something. Therefore to describe a dog's behavioural problem as aggression is largely inaccurate. It's a bit like saying that diarrhoea is a medical condition, when actually it's not. It's a symptom of what could be a number of different medical disorders and is not therefore the root cause. In the same way, there are a number of things that can prompt a dog to use aggression and in many cases it

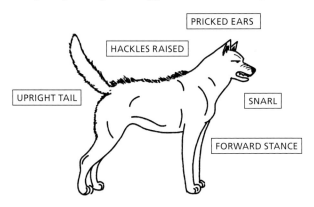

Fig. 4.1. Offensive Aggression: General Body Postures and Signalling.

Opposite: Photo courtesy of Tommy Taylor.

stems from fear. In fact, studies show that fearful dogs have a much higher likelihood of using aggressive behaviour when compared to non-fearful dogs and this poses a risk, not only for the dog in question but also for the health and safety of others.

Types of Aggression

Offensive aggression is a more assertive form of aggression (Fig. 4.1). Dogs will generally adopt a more forward stance, with pricked ears and an upright tail, often making eye contact in order to intimidate. These dogs bare their teeth and use threatening vocalizations to inform the opponent that they mean business.

Defensive aggression is the type of aggression mostly associated with fear (Fig. 4.2). In contrast to offensive aggression, dogs tend to shrink back with the tail lowered and tucked close to the anus. At the same time they can exhibit aggressive behaviours such as growling, lunging and snapping, sometimes advancing and then retreating. The best form of defence, in some situations, can be to attack and so a dog will escalate to offensive aggression if the threat gets closer and they continue to feel threatened.

Fear-aggression is closely linked with defensive aggression. It can usually be identified and diagnosed when a dog shows hostility to something or someone it encounters that they are afraid or uncertain of. Problems arise when fearful dogs learn that aggressive

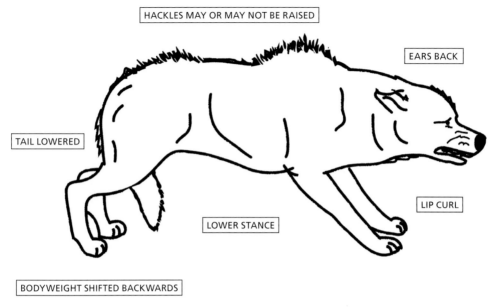

Fig. 4.2. Defensive Aggression: General Body Postures and Signalling.

behaviours ward off the fearful stimulus and soon they begin to default to aggression as a coping strategy. Fear-aggression very often stems from lack of proper socialization or because of a previous, traumatic experience.

Frustration-elicited aggression typically occurs when a goal cannot be achieved. For example when the dog feels trapped, unable to retreat or is unable to take action.

Pain-induced aggression can be seen in even the most placid dog. Aggression becomes more likely when they are handled or approached. There is some crossover with defensive aggression because they are, in a sense, protecting themselves from further pain.

Redirected aggression occurs when a dog is unable to direct aggression to the target of their hostility, perhaps by being restrained on a lead or looking through a window. Once in a state of heightened arousal they may bite someone else or another dog close-by on impulse. Redirected aggression often occurs during dog fights, when an owner tries to intervene and inadvertently gets bitten.

It can be hard to understand that a dog is frightened when the main presentation is that of aggression. This is especially so when an adopted dog enters a new home as an adult and is already using aggression as a way of coping with fear. Similarly, younger dogs can start to use bolder and more proactive behaviours as they mature or when

going through a developmental stage and this can come as quite a shock to an owner, particularly if earlier, subtle signs of fear and appeasement went unnoticed. Very

Health and safety is important to protect members of the public and safeguard the dog. (Photo: Rhea, courtesy of The Yellow Dog Project)

What to Do When a Dog is Showing Aggression

- Get the dog checked by a vet to eliminate pain and medical problems.
- Seek professional help from a recognized and suitably qualified canine behaviourist as soon as possible.
- Begin muzzle training (*see* 'Muzzle Training', Chapter 10).
- Ensure the safety of others; stop taking the dog out to public places until help can be sought or make sure that they are safely under control and wearing a well-fitted muzzle.
- Protect visitors to the home. Postal workers, utility providers and other authorized visitors to your property should be able to carry out their work without encountering and feeling threatened by a dog.
- Ensure that your garden is secure to reduce the likelihood of the dog escaping and also to prevent trespassers. Under UK law, owners may be liable if a dog injures someone trespassing on their property.
- Take steps to understand the legal position in the country where you live. Even when the dog's underlying motivation is fear, there are legal implications of owning a dog that shows aggression.

The Escalation of Aggression: (a) Lower level stress signals.

The Escalation of Aggression: (b) Alert and aroused.

often these owners report that the aggression began suddenly, when in fact they just weren't aware of, or didn't quite understand, the dog's earlier signals.

The Escalation of Aggression

A fearful dog moves from mild, low-level stress signals, which are designed to avert threat, to more heightened forms of overt aggression as it feels more intimidated. This concept was described by Kendal Shepherd, a veterinary behaviourist, in an illustration called the 'Ladder of Aggression'. The more subtle signs of stress were depicted on the bottom rungs of the ladder and the more overt signals were expressed at the top. However, our actions can affect the outcome. If we choose to respond earlier in the sequence and take the necessary action,

The Escalation of Aggression: (c) Heightened defensive aggression. (Photos: Jessie, courtesy of Amy Crossley)

55

we can avert a rise in aggression and diffuse a situation quickly. Conversely, if we don't, aggression escalates further. Through learned behaviour a dog may discover that more advanced forms of aggression work more effectively in repelling a threat and turn to these more proactive behaviours much more rapidly, skipping some of the early warning signals. These dogs are then described as being unpredictable and impulsive when, in fact, their behaviour was entirely predictable.

Trigger Stacking

A trigger is something that sets off a memory or is associated with a fear-inducing stimulus or event. Triggers are activated through one or more of the senses: sight, sound, smell and, perhaps to a lesser extent, touch. Trigger-stacking is the term given to stress accumulation and the more negative triggers that a dog encounters, the greater the probability of an antagonistic reaction (Fig 4.3).

Mood State

Moods are influenced by internal and external environments such as hormonal activity, pain and things going on in the outside world. As such, moods fluctuate. It goes without saying that people have different mood states and this is usually an accepted part of being human. It's extremely common for someone to act out of character when they are feeling in a low mood and more to the point we usually acknowledge, and most of the time can forgive someone when they have a bad day. However, we sometimes forget, and seem less willing, to accept that dogs and other animals have mood states too. Given they are mammals and share a similar biology to us, it seems

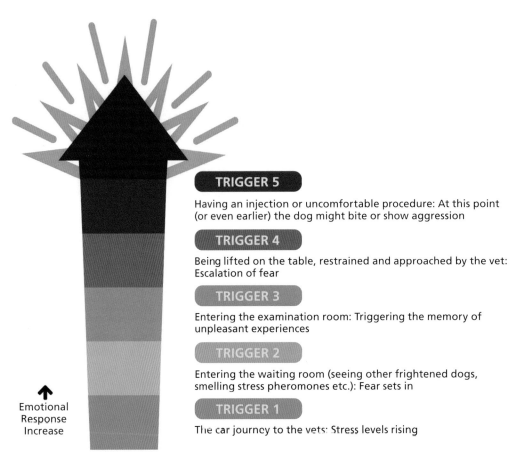

TRIGGER 5

Having an injection or uncomfortable procedure: At this point (or even earlier) the dog might bite or show aggression

TRIGGER 4

Being lifted on the table, restrained and approached by the vet: Escalation of fear

TRIGGER 3

Entering the examination room: Triggering the memory of unpleasant experiences

TRIGGER 2

Entering the waiting room (seeing other frightened dogs, smelling stress pheromones etc.): Fear sets in

TRIGGER 1

The car journey to the vets: Stress levels rising

Emotional Response Increase

Fig. 4.3. Trigger stacking: Negative triggers affect mood states singularly but when stacked up may affect a dog's ability to cope. Intervening early in the sequence can avert problems.

perfectly plausible that mood will be a factor in how a dog reacts and expresses their fears and anxieties at any given time. Nevertheless, sudden displays of aggression without any obvious cause should be investigated and not ignored.

Castration and Aggression

It is beyond the scope of this book to have a thorough review of how sex hormones and neutering affect the dog's behaviour and health. Yet, because castration is sometimes advised for male dogs, based on the assumption that it will stop aggressive behaviours, I feel I should include some information on this topic and dispel some commonly held beliefs.

Testosterone is a hormone produced primarily in the testes of the male. It's responsible for stimulating some of the male characteristics and driving sexual behaviours such as roaming in pursuit of a female, urine marking and mounting. One of the common myths about testosterone is that it renders all male dogs more aggressive and that castration (surgical removal of the testes) will stop a dog displaying aggression. This is not entirely the case.

Certainly, testosterone may well lead to aggression if two entire (uncastrated) males are competing for access to a female dog in season. Also, if an entire dog is already aggressive, he might escalate his aggression more quickly, be poised for the next bout of combat more readily and take longer to return to his baseline state than he would if he had been castrated. But, to be clear, testosterone doesn't make a dog aggressive per se and castration isn't a cure all.

First, we must remember that all behaviour is influenced by learning. So if a dog has been using aggression to deal with a given situation for some time, castration alone isn't likely to help. Also, mounting can be induced by stress or may be used as part of an attention-seeking method. So these behaviours may not necessarily be driven by testosterone.

Turning our attention back to the fearful and nervous dog, castration may actually exacerbate their problems. This is because testosterone is also associated with giving a dog greater confidence and reducing fearfulness. Consequently, removing testosterone through castration could theoretically make them more nervous which might, in turn, increase the risk of fear-aggression. Nevertheless, castration might help in cases where a dog is showing competitive aggression towards other male dogs, escaping to get to females and mounting other dogs, people and objects in a sexual nature. It might also be a recommendation on medical grounds. However, this can be a dilemma if the dog in question is fearful and anxious.

Where possible, it is always better to address the dog's fear-related problem before rushing into surgery. Only when the dog begins to respond to a behaviour treatment plan should castration be considered. Chemical castration (an implant given under the skin) is another alternative to surgery and, because it is reversible, might be a better option. Consult a veterinary surgeon to discuss a plan of action.

Frustration-elicited Aggression

Most of us will have experienced frustration ourselves so we can perhaps appreciate how it can make a dog feel stressed, angry and uptight. Here is an example of a situation in our human world that might help to illustrate the effect that frustration has in terms of a dog's mood state:

> We buy a piece of flat pack furniture and the box says 'Easy to Assemble'. Our expectation is that we should be able to erect it easily! Three hours later, we are no further ahead with assembly. Most of us will be feeling frustrated. The expectation hasn't been met. Another three hours later and the furniture has been thrown on the floor, we are stressed and in a negative emotional state. We then redirect our frustration to the closest person and end up having a blazing row with them. We feel annoyed, irritable and our threshold for aggression is low.

Typical behavioural signs of frustration in the dog include:

- High arousal including the typical physiological changes (for example dilated pupils, increased respiration rate).
- Aggressive displays such as snarling or growling to communicate the desire to be left alone or to take a particular action.
- Pulling or lunging, usually in an effort to escape or ward off the approach of something frightening.
- Vocalization.
- Redirected behaviours such as grabbing the owner's wrists or lead if the goal cannot be achieved.
- Displacement behaviours, for example spinning, over-grooming or other out-of-context behaviours.

Frustration and its Role in Fear-Related Behaviour Problems

For dogs with separation anxiety, being left alone, unable to escape and denied access to the owner or their attachment figure can be the cause of great frustration. When coupled with fear this can be an overwhelming combination, leading to destruction and even redirecting and causing self-inflicted harm.

Being unable to avoid something unpleasant or not having control over the environment is another trigger for frustration. This is typical for dogs at the veterinary clinic. Despite their best efforts at trying to communicate that they would prefer to be left alone, by using appeasement signals and struggling to escape from being restrained on the examination table, their attempts are thwarted. The outcome of this is often fear-aggression.

Frustration is likely to be experienced by dogs that are fearful of strangers or other dogs too, especially when out on walks in busy places. This is usually because attempts at repelling or escaping from them are unfulfilled. Some dogs react by spinning on the lead, whilst others may redirect their pent-up frustration towards the owner by mouthing them or biting the lead. Indeed, owners often report that their dogs are less problematic when they are off-lead. This is probably because they have the freedom to escape and put distance between themselves and their target of concern.

Being able to take decisive action gives the dog some control, which relieves their fear and frustration. Unfortunately, off-lead walking isn't always a possible or safe option but we can help out. Managing their environment by going out to quieter places at quieter times and thinking about creating a satisfactory distance from the target of their concerns are easy ways to reduce some pressure for them and for us. This isn't always easy and in Part II, I shall be covering some suitable management and treatment strategies to help with this problem.

Types of Frustration

In many cases frustration is context specific, and this is often known as state level frustration. In other words the behaviour usually only occurs in certain circumstances or within certain environments. In some ways this can be easier to deal with as triggers can be managed better. However, frustration can also be a temperament trait. In other words, some dogs may be more prone to trait level frustration. This might be a characteristic inherited from the parents but may also be a learned behaviour. For example, if a puppy was never taught to wait for a resource or a reward, they may not have the tolerance or emotional resilience to cope with delays or denials. This can give rise to frustration intolerance and can, in itself, be the cause of stress.

This same response might occur if a dog was not socialized appropriately. For example, they may have attended puppy parties or had experiences where the majority of interactions with other dogs involved off-lead riotous play. Therefore their expectation is that, upon seeing other dogs, they can gain access to them to play. When this expectation isn't met, because of being on the lead, the young dog gets frustrated and wound up, barking, spinning and generally over-reacting. This is very often wrongly interpreted as dog-dog aggression when, in reality, it is something quite different. More importantly, so is the treatment. Moving away, instead of bringing the dog relief, is a punishment. Therefore, teaching a calm, focused behaviour and putting it on cue means this can be requested before the frustration escalates. The dog is then rewarded by moving towards the other dog, such as a friendly 'stooge' dog in a controlled setting, or if that isn't an option, they receive food or play for their more appropriate, focused response.

It is important not to set our dogs up to fail so we must ensure that, during the socialization period and beyond, they are taught to meet other dogs and people on lead as well as off-lead in a polite and sensible manner. It's not compulsory to meet all dogs and training must include passing other dogs without making contact so that they learn to ignore them when they need to. Some frustration reduction techniques can be found in the training guides in Chapter 10.

Training that incorporates focus and control can help build frustration tolerance. (Photo: Millie and Caroline, courtesy of Tommy Taylor)

A reactive dog is difficult to control and handle. (Photo: Sky, courtesy of Leanne Miller)

The Reactive Dog

One of the most challenging facets of fear-related problems is the dog's level of reactivity. Highly reactive dogs tend to be more impulsive and they don't process information in a measured way, often responding without considering the consequences. The more reactive and impulsive they are, the more difficult it is to intervene and redirect them. Even more challenging is when a highly reactive dog has a low tolerance for frustration because, if not managed properly, it almost always leads to aggression. The highly reactive dog typically has a low threshold for reactivity, a short window of time in which they can be diverted or redirected to engage in another behaviour, and reaches their maximum reactivity level rapidly. Behaviours in reactive dogs can appear similar to frustration and this may well be a motivation. Signs include dramatic barking, growling, snapping, lunging, spinning, pulling on the lead and rearing up on their hind legs. Teaching a dog or trying to modify its behaviour when it is in this emotional state is virtually impossible because of the high levels of cortisol and adrenaline flooding their system.

In settings that trigger a reaction, highly reactive dogs spend a lot of their time thinking about or being reactive. This unfortunately reduces the opportunity to teach them new and more appropriate behaviours. Compounding the problem further is behavioural sensitization, which renders the dog more responsive to other triggers going on in the environment. Changing or modifying the environment is therefore a very important part of treatment

Lunging and barking are common features of high reactivity. (Photo: Jessie, courtesy of Amy Crossley)

because this invariably reduces the dog's arousal levels. For some dogs, in the short-term, stopping being taken to places that elicit their reactivity altogether would be wise, especially if they pose a danger to others and they are continually repeating the same modes of behaviour, not to mention feeling in a negative emotional state.

Replacing exercise with mental activities in the home and garden would help to fill a gap and hiring an enclosed dog-walking field, where the dog can have the place to themselves, relax and carry out the usual canine activities like sniffing and exploring will help to reduce tension and provide a better foundation for behaviour modification. During the period of relaxation, other work can begin and time can be spent wisely practising using different, more appropriate, training aids, honing training skills and following a targeted behaviour modification plan under the guidance of a professional.

Inadvertent and Self-Reinforcement

Dogs that use aggression and high reactivity may gain relief if their behaviour is successful and this could encourage and reinforce them to repeat the same behaviours in the future. In other words if their reactions result in the desired outcome (for example to make the frightening thing stop or go away) then they will continue to use the same behaviours to deal with it in the future. On the other hand, this shouldn't deter us from removing the dog from a situation. The key is to know *when* and *how* to manage and intervene appropriately so we can help break the cycle of events.

Knowing When to Intervene

Knowing when to intervene in the sequence of events is important. We have already touched on how we should intercede when a dog communicates their fear through their body language and understanding how this can escalate through the concept of the ladder of aggression and trigger-stacking is useful to know too. For the reactive dog a similar approach is required. Typically, they stiffen, stare and shift their weight toward the trigger. Somewhere in that sequence, the dog's behaviour will make a rapid transition into reactivity. Once that level has been reached it is virtually impossible to teach them anything and so it is better to protect them and get them out of the situation quickly.

The best time to intervene would be before the transition to reactivity occurs (Fig. 4.4), but, to be meaningful, the dog needs to see the focus of their reactivity and

Timmy's Tale of a Self-Reinforced Behaviour

Timmy, a four-year-old neutered Border Terrier, was extremely reactive when delivery people came to the house. Over the years, Timmy's behaviour had progressively got worse and almost on a daily basis he was in a state of high reactivity. He would jump at the windows and door, barking and snarling aggressively. Sometimes Timmy would snatch a letter as it fell through the letter box and redirect his aggression towards the mail by tearing it up. His owners were worried that if he managed to get outside, he would bite someone.

In cases like this, a dog is reinforced by their behaviour because when they bark aggressively, the delivery person goes away. Consequently, in the dog's mind their behaviour has been successful.

Methods of dealing with this case should primarily centre on control and management. This might include fixing letter and parcel boxes to gateposts or walls that are some distance away from the front door. Closing curtains and shutting blinds will also put a stop to the visual trigger. Once this has been done, steps can be taken to change Timmy's emotional response so that in the long term he feels more positive about delivery people.

learn that nothing bad came of it. This forms the basis of a technique called counter-conditioning and later in the book we shall be looking at how this method can be used to help these dogs.

Habits, Habits, Habits...

Habits can become an added complication in many behaviour cases, particularly with regard to aggression and high reactivity. Habits are deeply rooted behaviour patterns, learned over time. When the dog practises a particular behaviour over and over again this leads to the development of strong neural pathways in the brain. With repetition, these neural connections strengthen until eventually the undesirable lunging and barking behaviour becomes almost automatic and may be

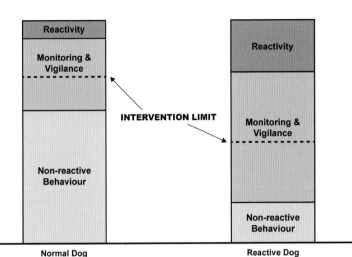

Fig. 4.4. The intervention limits of a normal and reactive dog. The intervention must come before the dotted line. (Adapted from Overall, 2013)

A trigger for fear-aggression can be seeing unfamiliar people approaching the house. Removing visual stimuli is an early management step. (Photo: Jazz and Chester, courtesy of Joanne Tarling)

behaviour, by intervening at the right time, can help. Also teaching them new, more fulfilling and enriching alternatives helps them make more appropriate behavioural choices and, over time, these become the new habits and overtake the old ones. In this way the dog (and owner) can move towards leading a more full and normal life.

Key Take Home Points

- Fear and frustration are common underlying motivations for aggression.
- Trigger-stacking affects a dog's mood state and can affect their ability to control aggression.
- Castration is not a guaranteed 'cure' for aggression and may make the behaviour of fearful dogs worse.
- Low frustration tolerance and high reactivity are linked to aggression.
- Responding appropriately and early in the sequence of fear can interrupt and lessen the development and escalation of aggression.
- Repeating inappropriate behaviours can lead to habit formation.

---

less motivated by an emotional state or goal and more from an unconscious learned response. A significant part of helping these dogs therefore is preventing these behaviour patterns from taking root. Managing their

CHAPTER 5

Preventing Problems

When it comes to safeguarding a dog against fear-related problems, the old adage 'prevention is better than cure' is extremely apt. Because a puppy's early life experience has a major impact on their emotional development, breeders should take the necessary steps to ensure they act responsibly and prospective owners should know the questions to ask and what to look for to avoid the pitfalls. Helping a dog get off to a fear-free start in their new home and knowing how to proof against some of the more common problems decreases risk and is a key factor in improving a dog's life. These are the main themes of this chapter, although many of the preventative measures discussed can be modified and adapted for the adult dog too.

Despite their working background, Greyhounds do not require high levels of physical exercise. (Photo: Penny and Asha, courtesy of Sarah Pugh-Hardy)

Preparing to Get A Dog

The choices that are made when thinking about getting a dog are important in preventing problems and this invariably relates to the type of breed that an owner chooses. Doing some research on what the breed was selectively bred for is important. You might wonder how this relates to fear and anxiety, so let me expand. Some breeds are more suited to a sedentary lifestyle whereas others were bred to work and to do a job. Don't be fooled though. Some dogs that are associated with high energy, such as the Greyhound, bred to course game and race, can be very laid back and don't require that much exercise. Nonetheless, certain working breeds, especially if bred from working parents, are more likely to have high mental and physical energy demands.

Deprived of an outlet, these dogs may well divert that energy towards other behaviours. Without much to think about or do, they can begin noticing and attending to stimuli in their environment that in other circumstances they would have ignored. Noise sensitivities can develop and bottled-up energy can sometimes spill over when busy owners eventually have time to take the dog out. This can lead to high arousal and reactivity towards things going on around them, which can be compounded further if the dog has a predisposition for being nervous or fearful.

Of course problems such as these can arise in all breeds of dog and mental and physical enrichment is a crucial requirement for any breed but when dogs, particularly those that were bred to work, haven't got anything to accomplish or achieve there is a higher risk of them developing behavioural difficulties.

Remembering that certain breeds may be more prone to certain behaviours means their training needs can

OPPOSITE: Rollie, Alfie and Jessie, courtesy of Amy Crossley.

To prevent boredom and the development of problem behaviours, working breeds can be given mentally enriching activities. (Photo: Rufus, courtesy of Amy Clark)

Border Collies have a high predisposition for sound sensitivities and herding behaviours. (Photo: Jessie, courtesy of Amy Crossley)

be met early on. As well as an apparent prevalence for sound sensitivities, the Border Collie and other herding breeds can redirect some of their innate behaviours to chasing cars, joggers and cyclists. Although this behaviour might not in itself seem to be related to fear and anxiety, it could potentially lead to fear conditioning if people retaliated aggressively or if the dog was injured in pursuit of a car.

In relation to pain and its link with fear-related problems, doing some homework on what health conditions a particular breed is predisposed to is sensible. For some breeds, health screening is available for certain hereditary disorders, so breeders should be asked whether the parents have been checked and are free from any problems that can be passed on. For example hip X-rays can be assessed and scored for the presence of hip dysplasia, a painful condition that affects the development of hip joints and leads to arthritic changes. In the UK, the Kennel Club (KC) provides comprehensive information about the health-related problems for all KC registered breeds and their database contains tests and results carried out on the parents of a litter. This is a resource worth using in order to gain proof of what tests have actually been carried out.

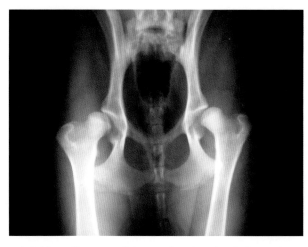

Painful hereditary conditions such as hip dysplasia can be prevented by screening dogs before breeding from them. (Photo: Holly)

Visiting the breeder in advance gives an insight into how and where the dogs are housed. This helps to ensure they are in an enriched environment and that they are stimulated by a range of different sensory experiences. Some dogs that have been reared in the countryside or who are housed in a separate location to the house can, if not socialized and habituated properly, have some problems adapting to life in a normal household or in an urban town or city. Checking what measures the breeder has taken to ensure puppies have been prepared is important. As previously mentioned, meeting the mother is essential. She should be friendly and confident. If she is reactive, fearful or wary about approaching you, this should act as a red flag. Remember that, through genetics and social learning, these traits are likely to be passed on to her offspring.

Commercial Breeding

Being able to recognize if a puppy came from a commercial breeder is crucial. These establishments operate on a large scale and are commonly known as puppy farms or puppy mills. Puppy farms tend to have low standards of care and there is a much higher risk of puppies being exposed to early life stressors. Not only that but the mother is unlikely to have had a relaxing pregnancy and so her stress levels will have potentially been elevated, affecting the puppy in-utero. A review of seven published studies undertaken by Franklin McMillian in 2017 found that puppies born in high-volume commercial breeding establishments and sold via the internet had an increased incidence of behavioural and emotional problems. This included aggression towards familiar and unfamiliar people and increased fear towards strangers, children and other dogs, when compared to puppies bred from non-commercial breeders.

Lucy's Law came in to effect in England in April 2020 and stipulates that all third-party sales of puppies at six months of age or younger are now banned. The law states that puppies have to be sold by the breeder, from the place where they were born and with the mother. The only exception to this is when a puppy is from a legitimate rescue centre. Unfortunately, unscrupulous people pose as breeders and, as a front, sell puppies from a house. In many cases, the mother isn't present and that should raise the alarm. Other warning signs include finding puppies advertised online with a number of different breeds to choose from and seeing the same pictures of puppies under different sellers' details.

Obtaining a puppy from a rescue shelter is hugely rewarding and saves lives. Nevertheless, spending the early weeks of life solely in a kennel environment is not an ideal start. Preferably puppies should be raised in foster homes with knowledgeable carers that create

opportunities for the puppy to experience social and non-social stimuli. If neither of those boxes can be ticked, a carefully planned socialization programme should be arranged as soon as possible.

Choosing a Puppy

Choosing a puppy can be the tricky part because very often it is our hearts that rule our heads. Obviously a puppy should look physically healthy but assessing their emotional health is important. A puppy's temperament can be assessed by watching them interact with their littermates and the mother. Puppies learn a lot through play, including bite-inhibition (how to moderate the strength of their bite) and how to deal with life's stressors. A confident puppy will greet a stranger and won't stay at the back of the litter looking apprehensive and frightened to approach. Gently touching a puppy all over and picking them up to see how they react can be another check. Obviously they should be supported safely and some wriggling is to be expected but they shouldn't try to mouth us and fend us off. Neither should they completely freeze

Emotionally sound puppies will be keen to interact in a friendly manner. (Photo: Puppies and Freddie, courtesy of Rebecca Wilkinson, Operation K9)

A Summary of Things to Consider When Getting a Puppy

- Choose a reputable breeder.
- Make sure the breed matches your lifestyle.
- Meet the mother (and sire if possible) to make sure they are emotionally sound.
- Assess the mother's attentiveness and maternal style.
- Look at the environment that the puppies and mother are kept in to ensure it is enriched and not too stressful.
- Assess the mother and puppy's temperaments.
- Ask pertinent questions about what socialization and habituation has been carried out.
- Ask about the mother's diet and what the puppies have been fed since weaning.
- Check that puppies from rescue centres have been socialized in foster homes.
- Check that any breed-relevant health screening tests have been carried out on both the parents.
- View the puppies more than once at different developmental stages.

In the UK, the Royal Society for the Prevention of Cruelty to Animals (RSPCA), together with the Animal Welfare Foundation (AWF), have developed a puppy contract, which is a freely available resource. This online tool encourages responsible buying and breeding of puppies and includes a template of a legally binding contract of sale. This resource is also available for breeders and demonstrates their commitment to responsible breeding practices. Guidance on how to access this is available in the Further Resources section at the back of the book.

and shut down. Although it might be a bit early in the pup's development to assess this fully, doing something slightly startling to see how they and, importantly, how the mother copes will be a useful test. Something fairly innocuous such as clapping your hands isn't too alarming but can help to assess how they react. It's perfectly acceptable for them to pay attention to the sound and maybe even startle a little. However, the puppy should

make a rapid recovery rather than make a dramatic run for it or freeze as if something extremely frightening has occurred.

Bringing A Dog Home

Getting things right from the start should be the aim. Bringing some of their bedding home with them will provide them with familiar scents and a sense of security. Feeding them the same food, at the same time they are used to, will help them retain a routine and prevents any gastro-intestinal upsets caused by sudden dietary changes, which can be an additional stressor. Even if you plan to make some alterations to their current regime, slow, gradual adaptations are best. As mentioned, a puppy should already have begun the process of habituation and socialization with the breeder but this must continue once they are in their new home. However, it's important to remember that moving from familiar surroundings, their mother and littermates will be stressful so taking it slowly and sensitively is important. If possible, collect the puppy earlier in the day so that they have time to adapt to their new home before leaving them at bedtime and limit the number of visitors to ensure they don't feel overwhelmed from the start.

If there are children in the house, it's important to educate them on gentle handling and to make sure they respect the pup's quiet space. If they are old enough, they should be taught how to recognize when a dog is frightened. Valuable information, pitched at a range of different ages, is freely available through a number of organizations such as the RSPCA, Blue Cross and Dogs Trust. Owners without children should make sure that they invite friends, neighbours and relatives with young families to come along and meet the puppy during their socialization period. However, most importantly, a dog should never be left with a child unless supervised by an adult. A sample of some of the experiences that a puppy should be introduced to during their socialization period is included in the Socialization Checklist in Chapter 10.

Fatigue affects behaviour in all ages of dog, especially the young puppy. Irritability, poor focus and lowered levels of concentration are just some of the effects, therefore puppies must be encouraged to have regular naps to prevent problems from emerging. Providing a designated space helps a dog identify the area as being safe and secure and they should be allowed to rest there without disturbance. As well as being somewhere to rest, a 'doggy safe space' can become their sanctuary during times of stress. Some owners choose to use a dog crate for this purpose and for short-term confinement, this can be a good idea, especially if there are small children in the house. However, confinement without the appropriate training can cause distress so crate training must be done sensitively and gradually (*see* 'Crate Training' in the training guides in Chapter 10). Crates should never be used to confine a dog as a punishment because this runs the risk of diminishing their positive appeal.

Diet

Nutrients and the composition of the diet influence every cell in the body including the brain and the nervous system. Without the correct nutrition, body systems don't develop or function properly and this will directly affect a puppy's ability to learn – a factor in how a dog behaves.

What to feed a dog remains controversial and is outside the scope of the book. However, for puppies, a high-quality, well-balanced growth diet, with ingredients that nourish the brain, is a necessity. Omega-3 essential fatty acid DHA (docosahexaenoic acid) is a key building block for neurological function and it has been suggested that feeding puppies a diet supplemented with fish oils, rich in DHA, from eight weeks of age, would improve their learning, memory and psychomotor abilities. One thing is for sure, good nutrition contributes to optimal brain function.

With regard to feeding behaviour, dogs weren't designed to eat all their food from a bowl in a matter of seconds. Therefore to ward against boredom and stress, mealtimes should be mentally stimulating. Scatter-feeding, hiding food and using puzzle feeders are great ways of channelling the dog's energy into an appropriate and fulfilling activity and this should be done from an early age.

Adopting an Adult Dog

Rehoming or adopting an adult dog from a rescue shelter can be extremely fulfilling. With a few modifications, the same principles for choosing a puppy apply. Speaking to the shelter staff helps, as they may be able to find a good match to suit a prospective owner's lifestyle. Sometimes

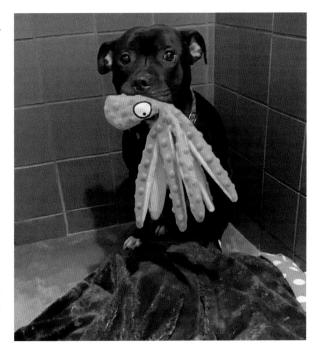

Adopting an adult dog can be extremely rewarding but being in a rescue environment may have been stressful so they will require a sensitive approach. (Photo: Gizmo, courtesy of Holly Barker)

the dog's full history and back-story is available and this can be valuable. Foster carers can also be a good source of information and tell you about the dog's behaviour. However, most adopted dogs need time to mentally 'decompress' after spending time in a rescue environment and it can take a while for them to settle in to a new home. Giving them time and taking a sensitive approach is important.

Dogs adopted from other countries, which have lived all or most of their lives as street dogs, are usually well proofed to meeting other dogs, but this might change once they are on a lead. Being denied the choice to approach another dog or retreat at their own bidding can be a source of stress and frustration. Another potential difficulty is making the transition to living in a busy urban home. Having never been habituated to a domestic scene, it can be overwhelming. So to reduce the risk of problems, it's advisable to begin as if they were a new puppy, introducing them to things gradually and incorporating strategies to induce relaxation. Better still, enlisting the help of a behaviour counsellor can help to map out a plan right from the start.

Recognizing Fear

As already discussed, a significant part of being able to prevent problems from developing is actually recognizing that the dog is feeling frightened or anxious in the first place. Studies have shown that owners don't always find this easy, especially when the dog uses more subtle, low-level stress signals. Under these circumstances, it's easy for owners to inadvertently push the dog beyond its ability to cope. Failing to read the signs not only means that the dog doesn't receive the help or comfort it requires but it can lead to flooding, which is the term used to describe prolonged exposure to a frightening stimulus at the maximum intensity and without any means of escape.

Preventing Separation Anxiety

Dogs are a social species and, given the choice, most of them would prefer to have some company. However, to prevent stress and anxiety, dogs do need to be able to cope with a degree of separation and isolation. It's natural for new owners to want to spend time settling in a new dog and taking time off work for a couple of weeks or so to do this is commonplace. Unfortunately, spending all day with them can become their 'norm' and afterwards, when the holiday is over, problems can arise because the dog hasn't been left.

As I write this we are just emerging from the global COVID-19 pandemic. Already mine and my colleagues' caseloads are flooded with dogs who are finding it difficult to cope with being left alone as things gradually return to normal and their owners are no longer available to be with them all day long. Because of the distress that separation issues cause, it's important to encourage autonomy from an early age. Breeders can begin the process by encouraging the mother to move away from her puppies for short spells. As well as giving her a bit of respite, it also means the puppies get used to being separated from their attachment figure. Also, being unable to suckle on demand is a good early exercise in teaching a puppy to cope with frustration.

Early habituation to isolation should be incorporated into puppy training, although it is important to do this very gradually and always return before they show any anxiety. This prevents the development of negative emotions associated with being alone. Also, if we wait until

Getting puppies used to being alone for short periods can prevent the development of separation-related issues. (Photo: Ralphy, courtesy of Sadie Fox)

they are crying for our attention before we return, we might inadvertently reinforce this behaviour.

Adopted dogs who have had a few different homes can be clingy and this can make them more prone to separation anxiety. Therefore it is important to introduce them to spending some time alone. Dogs tend to feel an owner's absence all the more if they get non-stop attention, so this should be discouraged. Instead, reward a dog for being calm and laying comfortably in their bed or when they are engaging in an independent activity.

Preventing Noise Sensitivities

Introducing a puppy (or adult newcomer) to a range of different sound effects, such as thunderstorms, fireworks and gunshots, whilst they are relaxing or engaged in something pleasant, is a good way of preventing the onset of noise fears and phobias. To replicate the sound accurately, the recordings should be of a high quality and played through a good sound system. Importantly the sound effect must be barely audible to us because their hearing is so much better than ours. This procedure follows the same principles of systematic desensitization (DS), a technique used to treat recognized fears. Gradual exposure to the sound is key and the dog must stay in a positive emotional state throughout. Going

Tips for Teaching Dogs to Cope with Separation

- Make sure they have a comfortable and safe place to relax.
- Use baby gates to prevent the dog from following and shadowing you.
- Encourage independence by giving them mentally engaging activities that they can do alone, such as interactive feeders, and praise them when they are engaging with them.
- Get ready to leave the house but instead of going out, sit and watch TV or do something else indoors.
- Monitor a dog's reactions to being left using a remote camera. The dog should be relaxed. Return if there are any signs of early stress.
- Very gradually increase the duration of time they spend alone.
- Incorporate these steps into everyday routines so they become the 'norm'.
- Get professional help promptly if the dog shows any signs of SA.

A baby gate can prevent puppies from shadowing an owner, helping proof against separation anxiety. (Photo: Irish Wolfhound puppies, courtesy of Anne Pope)

too fast, too soon can flood the dog and create a problem instead of proof against it. Veterinary behaviourists Sarah Heath and Jon Bowen have partnered with the Dogs Trust and made their range of high-quality sound-based treatments free to download. The link for this is available in the Further Resources section at the back of the book.

Finding A Behaviourally Aware Veterinary Clinic

As well as providing medical and surgical care, veterinary professionals also play a part in helping owners care for their pets' mental well-being. The veterinary clinic is often the first point of contact after a dog has been acquired and staff there should be able to offer advice on appropriate socialization, key developmental phases, as well as having the ability to pick up on potential or actual behaviour problems. Some vets specialize in behaviour

Things to Check Out When Looking for a Behaviourally Aware Veterinary Practice

- Does the practice follow low-stress policies?
- Are treats used in consultations to create positive associations?
- Is the dog given time to settle in the consultation room before being examined?
- Is the dog handled sensitively?
- Do the veterinary staff recognize when your dog is frightened and offer helpful behavioural advice?
- Does the practice provide opportunities for owners to drop by at a quiet time so the dog can receive a fuss and a treat from a member of the veterinary team?
- Does the practice offer puppy socialization classes (puppy parties)?
- Is the practice enrolled in any low-stress programmes?*

*The Fear Free certification programme for veterinary staff is an initiative founded by Dr Marty Becker DVM, a veterinarian and professor of behaviour based in the USA. Details of this can be found in the Further Resources section at the back of the book.

and can offer an in-house service, whilst others refer their patients to an independent practitioner. Either way, the practice has an obligation to offer or guide their clients to a registered professional who can provide accurate behavioural advice.

Puppy Parties and Training

Puppy parties, if run well, are a great idea, particularly when hosted in the veterinary clinic. This is because they can help to prepare a puppy for future visits without feeling any fear or trepidation. They also provide a perfect opportunity for puppies to socialize with a number of different people and interact and play with other puppies of a similar age in a safe environment. The emphasis should be on having fun but sessions must be structured and include valuable and positive learning experiences. Above all, they should be supervised by experienced and knowledgeable staff.

Play is encouraged at puppy parties, which is great, as long as it doesn't take up the whole session. As well as being introduced to other unfamiliar puppies, it helps a puppy learn communication signals, and enhances their life-skills. Ideally a play session should come towards the end of the class so that initial meetings and greetings are done on-lead. This is more akin to what they will be doing in the real world and helps to teach them frustration tolerance. But like children, dogs have different styles of play. Some are boisterous and vocal whilst others are reticent and quiet. This can lead to problems if a confident puppy is left to intimidate or frighten a less robust character and could be the trigger for the development of fears. Close observations are imperative.

Graduating to positive reinforcement training classes once the puppy parties are over is a good idea. A study to determine whether puppy training helped prevent behaviour problems later in life showed that aggression, compulsive behaviour, destructive behaviour and

Incorporating training at home helps to teach a puppy to look to us for direction. (Photo: Teddy, courtesy of Jordan Lapping)

Positive reinforcement training at an early age teaches a puppy some useful life-skills and can ward against the development of behaviour problems. (Photo: Ginny and Bex, courtesy of Christine Spencer, C S Canine Behaviour and Training)

Prior to vaccinations a puppy should be carried in order to ensure they are socialized to sights and sounds outside. (Photo: Rufus, courtesy of Amy Clark)

Harnessing the power of a dog's nose at a young age directs them to mentally enriching, appropriate behaviours. (Photo: Bramble, courtesy of Helen Milner)

excessive barking were all reduced in dogs that had attended puppy training before they were six months of age compared to a control group of dogs that had not attended puppy training classes (Dinwoodie *et al.,* 2021). Nevertheless, in order to teach meaningful lessons, building basic training into everyday routines is important too. For example, conditioning against frustration can be done by teaching a simple 'wait' cue before they access a meal or dash out of the door to go for a walk.

As well as finding a behaviourally aware veterinary clinic, other professionals such as dog groomers, boarding kennels and trainers should be chosen carefully. If planning to use a dog walker, enquiries should be made about the number of dogs they take out together. Not all dogs are well socialized and being mobbed by a large group of others that have poor social skills is a recipe for problems.

Key Take Home Points

- Many of the preventative measures for canine fear-related problems begin with the breeder. Choose wisely.
- Careful preparations can alleviate stress and help a dog settle in to their new home.
- Recognizing the signs of fear and anxiety help identify the onset of problems.
- Knowing how to proof dogs against common fear-related problems decreases the emergence of problematic behaviour.
- Choosing behaviourally aware vets and attending well-run puppy parties can help prepare a puppy for vet visits and teaches them important life-skills.

PART TWO

Practical Management and Treatment

CHAPTER 6

How Dogs Learn: The Laws of Learning

Teaching a dog to recognize and respond to cues such as 'Come', 'Stop' and 'Stay' helps keep them safe. Also, a well-mannered canine citizen can be taken to places with their owners and so they lead full and enriched lives. But dog training shouldn't only be to achieve obedience. Instead it should be about teaching meaningful life-skills so they can be sociable and well balanced, as well as shaping self-control so they are conditioned against frustration and impulsivity. Training gives the dog the means to access enriching and fun activities too but at the same time it encourages them to look to us for guidance, which promotes their sense of security. Training also brings a level of consistency and predictability to a dog's life, which are key components for preventing and treating anxiety. But, perhaps most importantly, for the dogs whose lives are filled with emotional turmoil, training gives us the power to change their lives for the better. However, in order to accomplish these outcomes we must understand how dogs learn. Learning theory can be a dry subject but once you begin to apply some of the practical elements of a training plan it will slot in to place. You might even learn to love it, like I did!

Learning and training go hand-in-hand. Learning is the acquisition of information and training focuses on the techniques that we use to bring about a predictable outcome. Learning can be non-associative or associative. Non-associative learning is the simplest form and doesn't involve any pairing between a stimulus and a behaviour. Examples include: habituation, sensitization and social learning, which have been introduced earlier in the book.

Like all animals, dogs are continually learning, even when we are not interacting with them or doing any conscious training. This includes things that we don't always

want them to learn. For instance, you may recall how fearful dogs can inadvertently learn that using aggressive behaviours makes the scary thing go away and how connections can be made with things that trigger intense fears, as we saw in Murphy's story back in Chapter 1.

In a nutshell, associative learning happens when dogs make associations between their behaviour and events. There are two main types; classical conditioning and operant conditioning.

Classical Conditioning

Classical conditioning was originally explained through work undertaken by the Russian psychologist, Ivan Pavlov (1849–1936). Under experimental conditions Pavlov presented his dogs with a neutral stimulus (a sound) immediately before giving them a meal. Naturally, seeing the food, and in anticipation of eating, the dogs salivated. After repeating this pairing, over time, the dogs began to associate the sound with the arrival of food and salivated just hearing the sound alone. Technically, responses that are not taught and just occur naturally, like salivating, are described as being unconditioned responses (UR), in other words they didn't require any prior learning to provoke a response. Yet, in classical conditioning, a neutral stimulus (such as a sound, an object or situation) can, by association, be conditioned to elicit a response and so become known as the conditioned stimulus (CS) and a UR then becomes a conditioned response (CR).

Don't worry too much about the technicalities. The main thing to remember is that classical conditioning influences how and what a dog learns. For example, a

OPPOSITE: Millie and Caroline, courtesy of Tommy Taylor.

Through classical conditioning the newspaper (now the CS) causes a negative reaction because of its association with punishment. (Please note: the newspaper was digitally added into the photo to illustrate the point.) (Photo: Rufus, courtesy of Amy Clark)

lead can cause a dog to be over-wrought with excitement but that's only because it has been repeatedly paired with going out for walks, which is pleasurable for most dogs. On the other hand, a set of door keys can conjure up negative emotions in a dog with separation anxiety because of their association with the owner locking the door behind them when they leave them alone. These are called conditioned emotional responses and it's being aware of this learning process that gives us an insight into how fears develop and how they are maintained. Nevertheless, classical conditioning can also be harnessed effectively in something called counter-conditioning, which is one of the most powerful training techniques we have for modifying a dog's behaviour.

Counter-Conditioning

As the name suggests, we are countering or opposing something the dog has already learned and so this technique is a reliable treatment for dogs that have already developed fear-related problems. To give an example of how counter-conditioning (CC) works let's take a dog

who is frightened of other dogs. Work begins when the dog is composed and relaxed. This is conveyed by their body language and other signals of calmness. They are then positioned at a distance far enough away from other dogs. Training may need to be set up in a controlled environment with 'stooge' dogs or somewhere safe, like a vantage point in a garden, or in a secure field. Every time another dog comes in view the trainer provides the dog with something extremely rewarding. So assuming that our imaginary dog loves chicken and cheese, they keep on getting those yummy treats, fed in abundance, whenever another dog appears. They don't need to do anything for the food because the overall aim is that seeing another dog predicts that something good is going to happen. Consequently, over time, their fearful emotion is replaced with more positive and pleasurable ones.

Consistency is key. If the dog doesn't get a goody whenever it sees something scary, progress won't be great. That's why you need to be well prepared with treats always to hand, just in case something happens outside of a formal training session. Alternatively, having another strategy up your sleeve to get away or control the situation helps to manage things when the unexpected happens.

Other reasons why CC might fail to work could be because the dog is not relaxed. In this case, simply creating more distance between them and the fearful stimulus could remedy the problem. On the other hand it could be that the dog isn't ready to begin training and needs more time to emotionally decompress, which might mean they require veterinary medication. Sometimes it's because the chosen reward isn't enough to compete with the scary stimulus. However, one of the most common reasons for failure is because the dog is making a connection with something else going on in the environment and that's usually because the person training the dog is getting the sequence wrong.

Importantly, the trigger (the scary thing) must always come just before the reward. If not, the dog might be making the wrong connections. For example, the trainer's hand going towards their treat pouch could predict the scary thing appearing. Or the actual reward itself can become the predictor of the scary thing if that precedes the dog seeing the trigger. So it is imperative that the dog being trained sees the trigger just before the reward. A word of caution – it will take time and patience before a dog is able to change their emotions and even longer to get to a stage where they remain in a positive state when the trigger is at close proximity. Sometimes, it's enough to expect the dog to cope well whilst you use another training strategy to move them to a safer distance. Don't expect too much too soon.

A dog can be counter-conditioned to traffic at a safe distance from the frightening stimulus. (Photo: Jenga, courtesy of Jemma Whitford, Ruffmuts Training and Behaviour)

Getting Things in the Right Order is Important When Carrying Out Counter-conditioning

1. The dog must be comfortable and below threshold before commencing the counter-conditioning training.
2. The dog must have seen (or sensed) the trigger *before* the reward is given.
3. The reward should be their favourite and given in abundance whilst the trigger is present.
4. Give food by hand or scatter a few pieces on the ground, always ensuring the dog stays aware of the trigger being present.
5. Do not ask the dog to offer a behaviour – just continue feeding while the dog is aware of the scary thing's presence and stop when the trigger goes away.
6. If the dog shows any signs of distress, hypervigilance or fear they must be moved quickly but calmly away.

In counter-conditioning, the ultimate aim is for the dog to begin to look to the trainer for the reward whenever they see the trigger (the horse) rather than reacting negatively to it. (Photo: Millie and Caroline, courtesy of Tommy Taylor)

Operant Conditioning

Operant conditioning is the other way that dogs learn. It differs from classical conditioning in that it is dependent on consequences. Put simply, if the immediate outcome of a behaviour is desirable, the frequency of the behaviour will increase. Conversely, if the immediate outcome is unpleasant, the behaviour will decrease (Fig. 6.1).

Reinforcement can be described as being positive or negative. Positive reinforcement (R+) involves adding something desirable to increase the frequency of a behaviour. For example, a dog is more likely to repeat a behaviour when it is followed up with the addition of a reward, such as a tasty treat, play or praise. This forms the foundation of reward-based training (Table 6.1).

Negative reinforcement (R-) involves taking something negative (undesirable) away to increase the frequency of a behaviour. In other words, R- strengthens behaviour by stopping or removing an unpleasant experience. Getting to grips with the idea of R- can be confusing because the word negative conjures up the act of punishment. However, punishment stops a dog doing something whereas negative reinforcement is designed to get the dog to do something. It also involves a reward structure whereas punishment does not.

To help understand negative reinforcement, it's useful to think about how car manufacturers use the process in order to get drivers and passengers to wear their seatbelts. They fit an alarm. It's that incessant tone that doesn't stop until we click our seatbelt into place. Once we do, the annoying noise ceases. Thus they have negatively reinforced us to wear our seatbelt. Electric shock collars work in a similar manner. Using the shock collar scenario, let's imagine a dog is prone to running away.

Once the dog strays beyond the allotted distance, the operator will sound a warning tone (which precedes the unpleasant sensation) via a remote-control device. To avoid the discomfort the dog will stop or turn back, the tone will cease and the shock (the punishment) will be averted.

I use this example merely to describe the process and don't condone their use. Quite the opposite. The problem with these devices, and other aversive aids like them (such as prong collars, choke chains) is that, in order for them to work effectively, the dog must know the pain is coming. That means that they will have had to experience discomfort at some point during the training phase. Another problem is that dogs can make learned associations with things that they happen to be doing or seeing at the same time as the unpleasant sensation is elicited which can lead to the emergence of new fears, worsen existing ones and cause fear-aggression. On the grounds of animal welfare, several countries in Europe have already banned their use, including Wales, Austria and Switzerland. England announced a ban in 2018, but challenges to the change in law have delayed legislative action (at the time of writing this book).

Although classical and operant conditioning work differently, when a dog is learning they are usually making unconscious associations between two things and are likely to be noticing the consequences of their actions. Therefore they are invariably entwined.

Reinforcers (Rewards)

Reinforcers can be categorized as primary or secondary. Primary reinforcers are related to biological processes (for example hunger) and include food, drink and certain tactile interactions such as stroking. Secondary

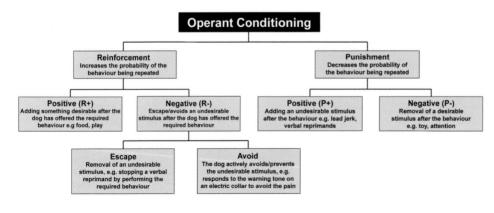

Fig. 6.1. An explanation of Operant Conditioning.

Table 6.1. Examples of the different aspects of operant conditioning (R+ and R-) and how consequences drive behaviours.

Antecedent (what precedes the behaviour)	Behaviour	Consequence	Outcome
You give a dog a recall cue	The dog returns	R+ Dog receives a tasty food reward	The behaviour is more likely to be repeated
You say 'Sit' whilst pressing on the dog's rump	The dog sits	R- you stop the unpleasant pressure	The 'sit' behaviour is more likely to be repeated

reinforcers are largely related to social conditions and include verbal praise and toys. They are also known as conditioned reinforcers because, as the name implies, the dog has to learn to associate them with something good. For example, a toy wouldn't mean much to a dog unless it had learned to associate it with play and praise is usually paired with something positive like touch or a treat.

Clickers, used in clicker training, are secondary reinforcers. A clicker is a small, rectangular plastic box that has a metal tongue inside it. When it is depressed and released with the finger, it emits a distinct and rapid clicking noise. Through classical conditioning principles, the dog learns to associate the noise with something rewarding, such as food. After a spell of foundation training, the click is used to mark the aspect of behaviour that is to be reinforced. So, for example, the dog sits, the trainer emits a click (to mark the desired behaviour) and the dog is immediately rewarded with food. A verbal marker, such as 'Yes' or 'Good', works in the same way.

Although I do use clicker training, I am a little hesitant to recommend it for fearful dogs, especially ones who are sensitive to sudden noises. Also, they require good timing and one hand needs to be kept free to operate them, not always an easy task when controlling a nervous or reactive dog. Nevertheless, in the right hands, and for some dogs, it can be a really useful training tool.

The nature of the reinforcer

It might sound obvious but for something to act as a positive reinforcer, it must have a positive effect. If a dog isn't too keen on cheese but that is the only thing on offer during a training session, they are unlikely to be motivated. Verbal praise and being stroked can also be rewarding but aren't usually enough to motivate a dog when they are

A clicker is a conditioned reinforcer and can mark the desired behaviour, although a verbal marker can be used instead. (Photo: Millie, courtesy of Tommy Taylor)

being taught a completely new behaviour or to maintain their enthusiasm. Using their usual food is not going to inspire them either, so always use high-value rewards during training sessions, especially when teaching them something new. Having a wide variety of rewards available during a session is a good idea too. Usual favourites include cooked chicken, sausages, liver and cheese. Variety helps the dog to stay focused and knowing that for a particularly great response they will receive their absolute favourite is a good motivator. Using an unexpected, high-value treat in this way is sometimes called a 'jackpot'. Used sparingly to reinforce a significant breakthrough in training, they act a bit like a gold star that a child might get for excellent work, spurring them on and encouraging them to succeed.

Studies have shown that animals tend to perform better for smaller, immediate rewards. Among other things, this is probably related to the fact that they do not get full quickly so they are kept motivated for longer. Another reason for using small pieces of food is that they are consumed quickly, so it doesn't interrupt the flow of the training session. For most dogs a small piece of food, about the size of a pea, is sufficient as long as it is tasty enough. Some trainers prefer to deliver treats via a tube to be licked from the end of the nozzle. Creamed cheese and meat pastes can be easily delivered and consumed quickly this way. Nevertheless, some dogs are not motivated by food and prefer play or to be given the freedom of being let off lead. For training to be successful, finding out what a dog likes best is really important.

Creating conditions that affect the efficiency of a reinforcer should be considered too. Food is less appealing after the dog has just eaten so it makes sense to time training sessions before they eat, although it isn't a good idea to withhold food for extended periods. Like some humans, being hungry can make a dog feel irritable and it can affect their concentration. Not a great state to be in for optimal learning to take place. Similarly, allowing a dog to have access to its favourite ball ahead of a training session would make it much less appealing if it was going to be used as the reward.

Training under threshold

As we know, the stress response can definitely get in the way of learning and performance. That's why people who suffer from extreme exam nerves don't do so well, even if they know their subject inside out. With this in mind, before we expect our dog to learn, we need to ensure they are calm and comfortable and under threshold. This is a term used to describe the point at which a dog's behaviour changes from a positive to a negative emotional state.

When a dog is under threshold, they are in a positive emotional state. They react within normal limits and are able to respond to cues. They can take food, play and feel relaxed and composed. In a training situation, they may be able to see, hear or sense the target of their fear, but it is at a level and intensity that they are completely comfortable with. This is the optimal time for learning.

When a dog is at threshold, they have reached the stage of noticing the frightening situation. They may become distracted and look or orientate in the direction of the object of their concern but do not show a significant fearful response. However, the changes and signs that take place at threshold can help predict that a dog's fear response is escalating and, for some dogs, the transition can be rapid. In the very early stages of training it is better to remove them calmly to a place of safety before they go over threshold, not forgetting to give them an abundant supply of treats, praise, play or whatever else they find rewarding for their compliance.

Once the dog goes over threshold they become completely distracted by the fearful stimulus and display signs of stress, failing to respond to cues. Although a few extremely food-orientated dogs may still take treats, they tend to snatch and consume them really quickly, often without taking their eyes off the target of their concern. At this stage the dog is not going to learn anything new. The fear response has been triggered and, in turn, inappropriate responses have been rehearsed and neural connections for the fearful behaviours have once again been strengthened.

The timing of the reinforcer

In addition to being above threshold, poor timing of the reinforcer (reward) is one of the main reasons why training may not appear to be working. To be effective, the reinforcer has to be delivered immediately after the response. If not, the effect can be weakened and the dog is unaware what they were being reinforced for. Worse still, another behaviour may inadvertently be reinforced. To help with timing, a verbal cue such as 'Yes' or 'Good' (or a clicker), can be used to mark the behaviour which can bridge the delay between the desirable behaviour and the reward. Nonetheless, practice really does make perfect. Dog training is a skill and unrehearsed training can

The Story of Joe and his Poorly Prepared Owner

Joe is an adult Boxer dog that is fearful of unfamiliar dogs. Whilst out for a walk with his owner, Joe sees a dog heading towards them. The owner effectively begins moving Joe in a different direction before he reacts. Unfortunately, they haven't really worked on their training skills and fail to offer any verbal praise (the secondary reinforcer) which would help mark the dog's calm change of direction. They're also finding it difficult to retrieve a treat (a piece of his dried food taken from his normal food ration) from their coat pocket. In the meantime, Joe's owner doesn't move far enough away and Joe has been able to turn back, barking and lunging towards the other dog, just at the moment the owner offers the food, which Joe snatches and quickly consumes. The owner recovers enough to lead Joe away for a second time and he begins to calm down. However, rather than being rewarded, Joe is reprimanded for his outburst and for snatching the food.

It's easy to see why things aren't progressing and why Joe is confused. Poor timing affects the strength of the reinforcer (as does the quality of the reward) and can inadvertently reward the undesirable behaviour. Worse still, being reprimanded for his desirable behaviour means he will be less inclined to offer it again in the future and is likely to have been an additional stressor. Poor Joe.

confuse and distract a dog. Joe's story (*see* box) is a fairly typical one and demonstrates why a dog fails to learn.

The Schedule of Delivery

Schedules of reinforcement relate to which responses will be reinforced and how often the reinforcer will be delivered. Continuous reinforcement (CR) means the reward is delivered for every single response and it's this schedule that is recommended when setting out training a new behaviour. In theory, once a dog has learned a behaviour properly, and is responding to the cue consistently in all types of environment, the schedule of reinforcement should be replaced with intermittent reinforcement. This means delivering the reward more sporadically, perhaps for every second or third response. This shift is recommended because a dog can become reliant on the continual flow of rewards, which discourages independence and affects their performance.

However, because we are working with fearful and anxious dogs, we should remember that they will probably be operating at the same level of difficulty throughout most of their initial training. My advice therefore would be to reward on a continuous schedule and get a good training manual, or seek help from an experienced trainer, to provide advice on when it's best to change the schedule.

One schedule that you do need to be familiar with is called a variable schedule. This one is used when following a programme of desensitization and features in treatment protocols for separation anxiety. As the name suggests it involves varying the length of time a dog is left and, although the aim is to desensitize them to being alone for longer periods, mixing things up a bit during their training is important. This way they are not able to predict if they are going to be left alone for a short spell or a longer one and so they don't get as anxious.

Punishment and its Pitfalls

In operant conditioning, if the immediate outcome of a behaviour is undesirable, the behaviour will decrease in frequency. Adding something unpleasant (for example shouting and physical punishment) is positive punishment (P+). Earlier we established that this and aversive styles of training are wrought with problems and are likely to make an already fearful and anxious dog worse and possibly aggressive. However, sometimes, owners and trainers find it difficult to know what to do to ensure a dog knows the difference between what they want them to do and what they don't want them to do.

Sometimes negative punishment (P-) is used to decrease a behaviour (not to be confused with negative reinforcement). This involves removing something desirable following a behaviour in order to decrease the likelihood of the behaviour being repeated and, done properly, is

Table 6.2. Examples of the different aspects of operant conditioning (P+ and P-) and how consequences drive behaviours.

Antecedent (what precedes the behaviour)	Behaviour	Consequence	Outcome
You lay on the sofa	The dog jumps on to the sofa	P+ you shout at the dog to get down	The behaviour is less likely to be repeated
You sit at the table to eat dinner	The dog begs for food	P- you ignore the dog and don't feed it	The behaviour is less likely to be repeated

humane and can work. Giving a time out, the withdrawal of our attention (which we might use to discourage the development of hyper-attachment) or taking away a toy when a dog misbehaves are all examples (Table 6.2). However, with fearful dogs we need to tread carefully.

Rather than using punishment we should provide a dog with the kind of feedback that works best and turn to reward-based training. One way of doing this is rewarding the dog immediately when they exhibit the behaviour we want. In dog training, this is called capturing. This is an extremely simple, yet reliable way of letting a dog know what they should do and, best of all, there is no need to use something too unpleasant (other than they don't get a reward). For example we might capture and reward a dog when they are relaxing in a den or settled on their mat and noise sensitive dogs might be rewarded if they ignore a noise in the environment. This type of regular, informal training soon gets the dog offering the kinds of behaviour we want voluntarily, which can be generalized in other situations.

Waiting for a problematic behaviour to arise means we are forced to deal with it in some way, whereas preventing it from happening in the first place allows us to dispense with correction. This can be achieved by managing the environment so that the dog has fewer (or no) opportunities to rehearse the problematic behaviour and, where necessary, an alternative, acceptable response should be taught to avoid frustration. Of course a blended approach is best but ultimately, setting a dog up to succeed is at the heart of good training and changing behaviour for the better.

Extinction... If I Ignore It Will It Go Away?

Extinction occurs when a behaviour that has been previously reinforced is no longer rewarded and, as a result, the behaviour diminishes. A simple example of using extinction is when we want to stop a dog from begging at the table. Having previously received titbits, we now consistently refrain from giving the dog any food when it begs. Eventually, when they realize that their behaviour isn't working, they will stop trying and the behaviour will be extinguished. Extinction may also be recommended if a dog's behaviour problem is developing or worsening by their attention-seeking, in which case we might advise the owner to ignore some of their actions.

However, a characteristic of extinction is the 'extinction burst'. This is a phenomenon that occurs when, once the dog stops getting the reward, they begin to try harder to get it. Consequently, the behaviour appears to get worse before it gets better. An analogy in humans is the child that throws a tantrum when the parent stops giving them sweets on demand.

Should I give in?

In most simple cases, no. Giving in just increases the ante. In other words, each time we bend under the pressure and give way, the dog will learn to keep increasing their efforts until they get the desired outcome and this just makes the problems get worse. So for straightforward behaviours, such as simple puppy play-biting, begging at the table and some forms of attention-seeking, extinction can work. Nevertheless, an extinction burst could lead to dangerous displays of frustration and doesn't teach a dog what to do instead. Therefore, it's far better, in tandem with extinction, to reinforce another more desirable, alternative behaviour to replace the problematic one. We shall be taking a look at the practical application of this and other training techniques later in the book.

Key Take Home Points

- Dogs learn all the time, even when we are not consciously teaching them anything.
- Dogs learn by association.
- In dog training we use the principles of classical and operant conditioning.
- For learning to take place, timing is important.
- Desirable behaviour must be rewarded generously and in a timely fashion.
- Rewards are only rewarding if the dog desires them.
- Positive punishment can backfire and lead to stress.
- Extinction works best if it is combined with teaching and rewarding a more desirable alternative.

Pet Education
& Training

Caroline Clark
Registered Veterinary Nurse, Cert.Ed, Full Member of The Association
Behaviour Counsellors, ABTC Registered Clinical Animal
www.peteducationandtraining.co.uk

Client Name: Amy Clark   Pet Name: Rio

Contact Details:

Behaviour Modification

Action	
1) Mental enrichment	To
2) fitness Training	

CHAPTER 7

Analysing and Modifying Behaviour

The role of the clinical animal behaviourist is to help owners change their dog's behaviour for the better and, in so doing, the lives of both parties can improve. To be successful, the dog must have been accurately assessed. Throwing a random collection of techniques at it, hoping that one of them will work is likely to fail. Analysing the behaviour in order to arrive at an accurate diagnosis is therefore a fundamental part of the process. This involves gathering as much information as possible in order to get a sense of what is going on. I often liken this process to putting together a giant jigsaw puzzle, with each small piece of information representing a part of the bigger picture. Considering all the evidence and having a clearer view of the problem means that a tailor-made behaviour modification plan (BMP) can then be contemplated.

Central to a positive outcome is appreciating the way in which a dog's environment affects their behaviour. Therefore, in this chapter, as well as sharing some of the methods I use to help me analyse a problem, I also highlight the importance of creating the optimal settings when planning behaviour modification.

Behaviour Analysis

As the name suggests, behaviour analysis is studying the dog's behaviour in a systematic way. In its simplest form it involves observing what the dog is doing and reflecting on their behaviour problem. However, that doesn't mean restricting observations to the actual fearful behaviour or limiting thoughts to what happened in the few

OPPOSITE: Rufus, courtesy of Amy Clark.

moments before, during and after their response to the fearful stimulus. It goes way beyond that.

Taking a History

Taking a detailed history underpins the whole process and questions about the dog's early life experiences help build a behavioural profile. Sometimes, for adopted dogs or those whose background is unknown, we might need to make some educated guesses and fill in some of the missing gaps. Getting a full account of a dog's current lifestyle can yield useful information. After the obvious information has been gleaned such as the age, breed and sex of the dog, the behaviourist will want to ask a wide range of questions relating to different aspects of the dog's lifestyle (Fig. 7.1).

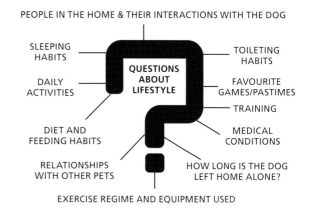

Fig. 7.1. Gathering information about the dog's current lifestyle is an important step in behaviour analysis.

Asking Questions About Diet is Important

We cannot underestimate the part that diet plays in a dog's behaviour. It is commonly accepted that there is a direct link between problematic behaviour in children and what they eat. Hyperactivity, poor learning abilities, changes in mood, and disrupted sleep patterns are just a few examples. The same is true in dogs. Attention should be paid to what colourings, preservatives and sugars a dog's current diet (and treats) contains, as these are sometimes the main culprits to problematic behaviours.

The types of question to ask yourself:

- Did a change in diet coincide with a change in behaviour?
- Is the dog's behaviour worse after eating?
- Are there signs that the dog may have a sensitivity or intolerance to the diet such as diarrhoea or skin problems?

Registered behaviourists will only work on veterinary referral so, with the owner's permission, they will be given the dog's medical history. This can be valuable because evidence of any past physical trauma or ongoing medical conditions may provide some useful and significant insight.

Using timelines

Once a dog's background and current lifestyle has been explored, the actual problem can be addressed. Timelines are a simple but effective means of gathering information. Basically, it's a list of important events arranged in the order in which they happened. When I am working with a client I usually draw a line on a piece of paper and use this to plot the development of the problem behaviour (Fig. 7.2). I find out when the behaviour first began and, if the owner can remember, all the events that preceded it right up to the present day. This can be a challenge but probing an owner with questions about what was going on around the same time such as holidays, birthdays, house renovations or other memorable events can help to jog memories. Very often this exercise provokes useful feedback, prompting recollections of how things developed and isolating a catalyst for the behaviour as well as ongoing triggers.

Once past events have been explored, we can then move on to the present. I like owners to give me a description of the behaviour in their own words; what it actually looks like and what happens. I try to encourage facts rather than a version of what they infer from it as this can confuse matters. For example, saying the dog 'behaves aggressively' or 'looks guilty' doesn't accurately describe a behaviour and can mean different things to different people. When imparting information it is more helpful to provide a detailed account of the event and describe facts such as the dog's body language rather than attempt to infer things from it.

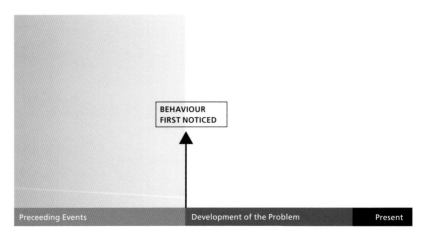

Fig. 7.2. A blank timeline (*see* Case Study 4 in Chapter 10 for a completed example).

I am also interested in the conditions under which the behaviour occurs as well as trying to analyse the function of the behaviour. In other words, under what circumstances is the behaviour most likely to occur and what does the dog actually gain from the behaviour? Conversely, but as important, I am also keen to hear about the occasions when and where the behaviour doesn't occur. Answers to these types of question help me understand motivations and maintaining factors.

The Antecedent Arrangement

When investigating a problem, and particularly when beginning to deliberate solutions, it helps to think more critically about behaviour patterns. You may recall from operant conditioning (Chapter 6) that it's the consequence that drives the behaviour and we can strengthen or weaken behaviours by using reinforcement or punishment. However, changing consequences isn't the only thing we can do to affect behaviour.

All the things that precede a behaviour are called antecedents. These are the events, actions, or circumstances in which certain behaviours are more likely to happen (Fig. 7.3). Analysing the antecedent means that, where necessary and if possible, they can be changed and, by so doing, we can deal with a problematic behaviour by changing the things that come before it instead of dealing with what comes afterwards. This means we can take a more proactive, instead of a reactive, approach.

Observing Behaviour

Observing the actual behaviour itself is an obvious part of the process but this needs to be approached with the same level of scrutiny. Let's imagine we are analysing a dog that is fearful of other dogs and, after being recently attacked, has begun to show some fear-aggression. The behaviour we might observe during a walk with this dog is him trying to pull the owner in the opposite direction as an unfamiliar dog approaches. As they get closer, the dog begins to bark, his hackles rise and then he lunges towards the other dog. After the other dog is led away, he begins to recover. But, in order to make a more comprehensive analysis we'd need to know much more. For example, we'd want to observe whether there were any subtle signals of anxiety much earlier in the sequence (even as early as him having the lead put on in preparation for the walk). Other noteworthy points of interest would include the type of equipment being used to walk the dog and how he was being handled. At what distance was the other dog before our dog showed any signs of arousal and what did the other dog look like physically? Also we'd want to know what sex the other dog was and did it convey any messages through its body language? What did the person walking the other dog look like and where was the dog being walked? How long after passing, or at what distance was the other dog before our dog settled to his baseline behaviour? Even observations about the weather conditions might be relevant (for example, some dogs are more reactive on windy days). And so on…

It's this level of detail that is of interest to the behaviour counsellor not only because it helps with getting the diagnosis right but it can be a springboard for designing a suitable behaviour modification plan. Armed with relevant information we may need to alter the type of equipment the dog is being walked in, change the environment where he is being walked and the way he is being walked. There wouldn't be much point working on desensitization and counter-conditioning (DS CC) with all dogs if our dog only ever reacted to entire male dogs, small

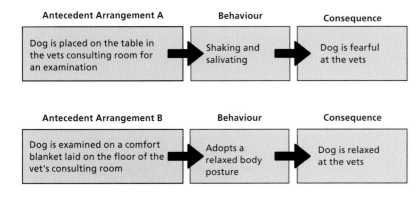

Fig. 7.3. A simple illustration of how changes to the antecedent arrangement can alter the dog's fearful behaviour.

brown dogs or dogs being walked by men with hats on. Can you see how it works?

Filming behaviour and logging events

Carrying out real-time observations isn't always easy for an owner, especially when they are in the drama. Things happen quickly, they are trying to cope with the problem and so their adrenaline is high, not just the dog's. A professional eye is often the most useful solution. However, videos taken without a stranger being present can be valuable for a behaviour counsellor to analyse, so getting family members or friends to help with recording is a

Doris – Same Dog, Different Behaviour

I was asked to help an owner with Doris, a three-year-old Labradoodle who was fearful of other dogs. After hearing all about the difficulties that the lady owner was having with Doris, and seeing some video footage of when she was taken out for walks, I then began questioning the husband, who I had requested to attend the session. He informed me that Doris hardly ever exhibited the behaviour with him. Further questioning revealed that he took the dog for the morning walk before he started work. This was at a very early time of day, when there were very few dogs about. Conversely the lady owner took Doris out in the early evening when there were more dogs being walked. She also reported that she was quite nervous about exercising Doris and later, during a test walk, it was clear that she was transferring her anxiety to Doris through the lead.

A lesson to be learned from Doris' story is to make sure that everyone who interacts with the dog shares their views and experiences. It also demonstrates how different interventions and modifications in a dog's physical and social environments can change behaviour. Being taken out at a quieter time, in a quieter place, with someone who handled her differently, affected Doris' behaviour in a positive way. Exploring and learning from everyone's experience can sometimes help to formulate a plan.

good idea. Playing them back can reveal things that might have been missed the first time around for an owner too and can be interpreted without emotional inference, provided they are watched when feeling relaxed.

Remote cameras can be beneficial and, for separation anxiety disorders, are essential pieces of kit. As well as helping to determine the period of time a dog can be left comfortably before the earliest signs of anxiety kick in, they can capture information that might help confirm a diagnosis. For example, a dog that has been vocalizing and damaging window frames may not be distressed at being left alone. They might be excited, alerted or frightened by seeing people, dogs or other animals passing by. Or they could be frustrated because they can't reach them.

Keeping a diary is also valuable. Once I have made an appointment to see a client I will suggest that they log their observations regularly. This can help us both see whether there are any recurring trends or themes that are affecting their dog's behaviour. Details of dates of when the behaviour occurred, how often and for how long the episodes last can provide meaningful data and, once a plan is in place, it can provide a benchmark to determine whether our interventions are having the desired effect.

Sitting down as a family and discussing the problem together is also beneficial. Each person's experience with the dog is different and this can throw up some interesting and valuable information, as my story about Doris demonstrates.

Identifying Triggers

I first introduced triggers in Chapter 4 in relation to trigger-stacking. These are the things that prompt a behaviour. Very often the terms antecedents and triggers are used interchangeably and there is crossover but don't worry too much about that. The main thing to remember is that analysing the setting conditions and observing things that precede and provoke the behaviour can be immensely useful.

Triggers can be absolutely anything but it's our powers of perception that really need to be honed to recognize some of the less obvious ones. Being acquainted with canine body language and signalling holds the key because these can provide useful clues as to the presence of a trigger in the environment. Formulating a list is a worthwhile enterprise because once they have been identified they can predict what might happen next and this allows us to intervene at the appropriate time. We may

Table 7.1. Examples of fear-related problems, the trigger that predicts the fearful event and ways to modify the dog's behaviour through manipulation of the physical environment.

Fear-related problem	Triggers that predict the fearful event and ignite the behavioural response	Examples of interventions we can apply in the dog's physical environment to help control the problem
Fear of thunderstorms	Sound of rainfall on a conservatory roof	• Move the dog to a quieter location in the house • Turn on the radio
Separation anxiety disorder	Owner putting on a work uniform in preparation to leave	• Owner waits until they get to work to put on their uniform.
Fear of visitors	Hearing the doorbell	• Replacing the doorbell with a sensor camera to see people approaching and intercept their arrival • Remove doorbell

also be able to remove them or manage them (Table 7.1) and, where applicable, for a long-term solution we can use them in their mildest form to carry out DS and CC techniques such as using recordings of fireworks or set up scenarios with 'stooges'.

Creating A Behaviour Modification Plan

Once behaviour analysis has been undertaken a behaviour modification plan (BMP) can be devised with greater clarity. Addressing the main issues and then breaking things down into manageable steps, gradually shaping the dog's behaviour in the direction we want by using positive reinforcement techniques and setting short-term goals, rather than fixating on the ultimate outcome, garners the best results. Nevertheless, changing behaviour isn't always easy.

As discussed, at the core of most fear-related problems are all the things going on in the dog's environment. Accordingly, to be successful, a plan should focus on altering what is happening there. Failure to do so makes behavioural change unlikely. However, what goes on in the dog's physical environment isn't the whole story (Fig. 7.4).

Modifying Environments
An effective BMP must also consider the social context of the environment. This includes all the social and socially related interactions that the dog has with other animals

and people. We have already seen how Doris' behaviour was affected by her owners' different handling techniques and we know that our actions and training methods can improve a dog's ability to cope. Interactions with dogs and other animals can't be ignored either. Things like the playing style between two dogs affects those individuals directly (and we can intervene if it's not positive) and social learning (from watching the mother or observing how other dogs interact), can also have an effect on what they learn, albeit indirectly.

There is a third type of environment up for manipulation and that is the dog's internal environment (also known as the neurochemical environment). This relates to what is going on physiologically. Interventions such as play, influenced by our social interactions, can enhance the production of feel-good neurotransmitters and prescription drugs and diet can affect brain and body chemistry too. Neutering can also impact the internal environment, leading to behavioural changes (not always for the better) as noted in our earlier discussion of testosterone. Even diseases can influence the normal neurochemical environment, leading to behaviour changes. In those circumstances veterinary interventions would be called for.

Altering a dog's environments is one of the first steps in modifying behaviour and a good plan must take these in to account. Sometimes, the changes we make may only be required as a short-term measure whilst the dog is undergoing training. At other times our interventions may be required as part of a long-term solution.

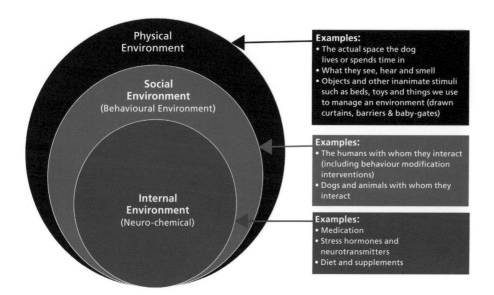

Fig. 7.4. The three environments that can be modified to change behaviour.

Simple environmental changes, such as moving a chair from a window or drawing curtains could alter a dog's awareness about something threatening from outside. (Photo: Ruby, courtesy of Karen Taylor)

Using Veterinary Prescription Medication

Throughout the book I have mentioned that some dogs may require veterinary prescribed medication to support their needs. This decision is largely based on whether the dog's welfare is being compromised or if their ability to learn is being hampered by their emotional state. Drugs can address these issues because they mostly work by increasing the availability of neurotransmitters (for example serotonin, GABA and dopamine) and act on the neural pathways involved in learning. In this way they modify the dog's internal environment. However, as with other additions to a plan, medication is not a silver bullet. Other behaviour modification techniques and environmental management still underpin the plan.

Some drugs are more suited to short-term situational occasions, such as a firework event or trips to the vets, and these work fairly rapidly. It's usually a good idea to do a trial beforehand because dogs can react differently to certain drugs and the dose rate might need to be tweaked. Other drugs are designed for long-term use and tend to take around four to six weeks to achieve their full therapeutic effects.

There are different classes of drugs and choosing the right one is a veterinary matter, although vets who don't specialize in behaviour will very often liaise with a clinical animal behaviourist to make sure the drug fits the case. One size definitely doesn't fit all and that's why a thorough behavioural assessment of the dog is required. Like any drug, there can be side-effects and, although problems are rare, the vet will want to monitor their physical health and a behaviourist will want to monitor their mental health.

One important point is, if the first drug of choice isn't effective, there are others to trial and sometimes a combination of drugs can have a better effect than one used on its own. Once a suitable regime has been found, a behaviour modification plan can be implemented with greater success and gradually the dog can be weaned off the drug. However, in some cases, for a dog's overall welfare, drugs may need to be given throughout their life.

Factors Affecting the Success of a BMP

Setting the right conditions is just one feature of a well-constructed BMP. Other elements would include selecting a suitable programme of training that teaches the dog alternative, appropriate behaviours using scientifically sound principles of learning. Setting the dog up to succeed is a major aim but this applies to the owner too. Organizing 'stooges' and finding private spaces might be the gold standard treatment for some cases but alas can be difficult to organize and may be costly. Being able to adapt and set up realistic alternatives, using other techniques can provide owners with a practical solution. A good behaviourist should therefore be flexible and work with the owner to design a plan to suit their routine, time budget, access to resources and skill-set. Otherwise compliance is likely to be poor.

A plan can be overwhelming if it isn't broken down into a series of bite-sized stages. Setting a series of tasks within each stage, and making sure that these have been fulfilled before moving on to the next stage, is the best approach. Demonstrating training techniques is something a behaviourist should do during the consultation and video tutorials and handouts can be useful additional resources to leave behind. However, regular check-ins should be arranged (some are usually included in the price of an initial consultation) so that ongoing support is available.

The first stage of most of my plans involves giving the dog time and space to relax without any pressure to face their fears. Getting them started with mental enrichment techniques is not too complicated and this can begin with immediate effect. During this period, owners can source any equipment needed and it also gives them the opportunity to practise their training skills (with additional help if required) as well as address any of their own emotional issues that might get in the way of the BMP. Successive stages are designed to build on each other, gradually progressing towards the end goal. A flexible approach is required because each dog progresses at different rates and there will always be blips along the way. Recognizing when to step back in a plan is one of the keys to success.

Even the best-constructed BMP is bound for failure if it is not implemented thoroughly. Unfortunately, there are no magic wands or quick fixes and change is often slow. We live in a world of 'press button', instant results but behaviour doesn't work like that. If a behaviour has taken months (and sometimes years) to develop, it's likely to take at least as long to learn a whole new way of behaving. It really is a case of being consistent and patient.

Owners will sometimes say they have tried everything and therein can lie the problem. Swapping from one plan to another in succession is never going to work. That doesn't mean that a plan can't be tweaked and sometimes I make some amendments based on the dog's progress. However, making sudden and dramatic changes to a plan is only likely to confuse the dog.

Being realistic about what can be achieved is something else to consider. Some dogs will always have special behavioural needs and it may be more a question of managing the behaviour rather than expecting a complete resolution of the problem. But, when you think about it, managing a behaviour successfully should stop the undesirable symptoms so in that sense, management is treatment!

Key Take Home Points

- Behaviour analysis requires close scrutiny of the problem and detailed questioning.
- Filming behaviours captures things that can be missed in real-time observations.
- Analysing and rearranging the antecedent arrangement can change behaviour.
- Identifying things that trigger the problematic behaviour helps us avoid or manage situations more efficiently.
- An effective BMP considers making changes to the dog's physical, social and internal environments.
- Each dog progresses at different rates and we should be led by their progress rather than setting strict deadlines.
- There is no guarantee of complete resolution for a behaviour problem although most can be improved with effective management techniques.

CHAPTER 8

First Steps

It's now time to think about applying everything we have covered so far into a behaviour modification treatment plan (BMP). This requires careful thought and planning. Working with fearful and anxious dogs can be challenging and potentially dangerous, so spending some time preparing and practising training skills is a necessity. Knowing where to start is sometimes the hardest part. Therefore, in this chapter, I have included some suggestions on the type of equipment to get hold of and how to use it. There are some useful core training exercises to work on too which will help when it comes to implementing some of the training techniques I have recommended. Being prepared includes considering our own mind-set, so I have a few helpful tips that can help alleviate our own stress before we take the training out on the open road. Step-by-step guides on all of the training techniques mentioned can be found in Chapter 10.

Health and Safety Matters

Health and safety have to be a priority, and knowing that a fearful dog might resort to aggression in order to deal with their fear means that all risks should be assessed and the relevant control methods put in place. In the UK, under The Dangerous Dog Act 1991, it is a criminal offence for a dog to be 'dangerously out of control'. This covers injuries to a person or animal as well as someone having a reasonable fear that they could be attacked. In other words, a dog doesn't necessarily have to bite someone for legal action to be taken.

It isn't uncommon for fearful dogs to snap and bite when startled and those that are fearful and highly reactive to other dogs might accidently injure the person walking them or redirect to other people close by. Owners are also liable if the dog bites someone on their property and, in some cases, even trespassers. Secure boundaries, signs on garden gates and the provision of letter and parcel boxes outside the boundary of the property are sensible measures. However, when out in a public place, to protect the dog, members of the public and the owner, suitable means of control and muzzle training should be high up on the list of priorities.

Muzzles

As well as preventing injuries to other dogs and people, a muzzle may be required for a number of other situations. This includes being able to carry out a veterinary or first-aid procedure safely and swiftly and, for the dog with fear of veterinary visits, having one already fitted at home prevents the trauma of being muzzled by the vet. Unfortunately, some owners object to using a muzzle because they are concerned that other people will think the dog is aggressive and that they may take a dim view of them. Yet, as well as the benefits outlined, keeping other dogs and people at a distance is precisely what many fearful dogs require. Being given a wide berth is going to help them feel more relaxed. So, in that sense alone, muzzles serve an extremely useful purpose.

Muzzles should be comfortable and well fitted but importantly should allow a dog to pant, drink and receive treats through the bars. Material muzzles that just encircle the snout, keeping the mouth shut, are not recommended other than for very quick procedures such as those carried out in the veterinary environment. Basket-style muzzles that are robust and can be cleaned

OPPOSITE: Millie and Caroline, courtesy of Tommy Taylor.

With positive reinforcement methods of training and creating positive associations with wearing it, over time, most dogs accept a muzzle quite readily. (Photo: Millie)

Muzzles should be used cautiously with dogs that have brachycephalic- shaped skulls, especially in hot weather. (Photo: Bella, courtesy of Sadie Fox)

easily are a good option. Certain brands are made of a hard, pliable material, which can be moulded to shape in very hot water before being fitted. These are more suitable for dogs with brachycephalic-shaped skulls (for example Boxers, Pugs and French Bulldogs) although, because these breeds often have compromised breathing, caution should be exercised when using them, especially in hot weather.

Training Aids and Equipment

There is an overwhelming range of dog-training equipment to choose from and this can be extremely confusing. Training aids on the market range from something as simple as a lead to devices that the manufacturers claim will instantly put an end to problematic behaviours such as barking, pulling and lunging. Needless to say, the last thing we should be doing is heightening fear by using something that issues pain or discomfort. Although any aid, no matter how innocuous, is ineffective and potentially harmful if used in the wrong hands. Despite the vast array of paraphernalia available to buy, there are surprisingly few essential items actually required. Here are some of the key items that are in my 'toolkit'.

Harnesses and Double-Clip Leads
Controlling a fearful dog safely and comfortably has to be a priority. Ideally the equipment should enable a handler to manoeuvre a dog quickly and lead them swiftly and comfortably to a place of safety. Unfortunately, the traditional lead and collar don't usually offer the right level of control and can put unnecessary pressure on the throat and neck, particularly in dogs that lunge, spin or pull on the lead. As well as causing discomfort and potential injuries to the vertebrae in the neck and the surrounding soft tissues, it can also interrupt the flow of oxygen to the brain. This interferes with their concentration and is likely to be a cause of alarm, exacerbating fear and reactivity. For these reasons, I advise using a fixed harness with two points of contact, one on the front and one on the back. These attachments are used in combination with a double-ended lead, which allows the handler to influence the dog's movements more easily and aids communication.

A little bit like reins, the double-ended lead makes it possible to alternate pressure and release between the two connections and this discourages pulling. The front attachment steers and guides the dog in a different direction rather than dragging them off-balance.

Meanwhile the back attachment helps to slow them down by a gentle upward lifting action of the lead. Pulling back should always be discouraged because, in the same way as pulling on a collar does, it prompts something called the opposition reflex. This simply means if you pull one way, a dog will pull equally as hard in the other, creating a tug-of-war type situation. Having the lead on both attachments helps prevent that happening.

The other benefit of using this arrangement is that the two points of contact make it easier for the dog and the handler to walk side-by-side. This is a much safer option than having a dog charging ahead, probably with the sense that they have to be in control, meeting challenges head on and managing social situations – a scary concept for most nervous dogs. In contrast, some dogs back away from something fearful and this can result in them slipping out from their collar and escaping. A well-fitted harness prevents this eventuality. Of course the dog still needs to be trained to walk loosely on a lead, using positive reinforcement methods, but this is much more easily achieved when the dog is comfortable, balanced and positioned beside the handler. Be cautious buying harnesses that are described as 'No Pull' as some of these are designed to tighten and inflict discomfort.

Now You Know How it Feels!

I have vivid memories of attending a Tellington Touch (TTouch) workshop where, to help demonstrate how a dog might feel on the end of a tight lead, we were asked to wrap both hands around our necks and exert pressure whilst reciting the eight times table. Maths was never my best subject so I tried it with the five times table – a tad easier! Even so, it proved difficult to do as I was so distracted by the unpleasant sensation. I can only imagine how much worse it would have been if I hadn't been in control of the pressure! This exercise really struck a chord with me and gave me a significant insight into the effects it might have on any dog, whether they had any underlying issues with fear or not. Try it yourself sometime, then you'll really see how it feels.

Choosing a harness

Care should be taken when selecting a harness because some can impede the normal range of movement in the forelimbs. Veterinarian and physiotherapist Dr Marianne Dorn recommends designs that have a Y-shaped front. These act mainly on the dog's breastbone at the front of the chest to promote a calming effect. Designs with a T-shaped front are not recommended because they apply significant pressure directly over the sensitive shoulder joints or surrounding muscles. She also advises that a harness should never extend beyond the dog's ribcage. Thin-skinned breeds of dog might be more comfortable in padded designs but, in all cases, look for harnesses with adjustable straps so they can be fitted snugly to avoid rubbing, pinching or chafing. Another thing to consider is how easy they are to take on and off. This is important for the nervous dog. Choosing one that has a variety of clasps means they can be dismantled which reduces the potential problem of looming over them or having to manipulate their legs into the straps, which can be perceived as a threat and, as Dr Dorn reminds us, can be painful for dogs with joint problems.

The harness that I am most familiar with, and one that fulfils these features, is the TTouch harness but there are others on the market and, because certain styles fit different shapes of dog better than others, it is worth trying out a variety of brands to see which one is the most suitable. Most manufacturers are happy to provide advice on fitting but check on their replacement and refund policies, especially when purchasing online. Like all new pieces of equipment, introducing a harness to a fearful dog should be done gradually

Y-shaped harnesses offer good control and do not impede the dog's movements. (Photo: Millie, courtesy of Tommy Taylor)

(*see* 'Harness Training' in the training guides in Chapter 10).

Double-clip leads

Double-clip leads come in a variety of widths and lengths, ranging from 1.5–3m (5–10ft) long. The size of the dog determines which one to choose. For my Labrador, I use a 3m (10ft) length. The beauty of the double-clip lead is that it can be used on both of the harness connection points for greater control or clipped on the back connector alone, allowing the dog more freedom to enjoy sniffing and exploring when they are in a safe space.

Practice is required because when used on both connections points it can feel a little strange to begin with. I recommend that this is done in the house or garden after a dog has already been exercised as this should help to get rid of their exuberance and aid concentration for both the dog and the handler. Practise changing direction, guiding from the front clip and slowing your dog down using the back attachment. Sessions shouldn't be any longer than a couple of minutes and praise and treats must be given to ensure the dog is rewarded for complying. Once the dog is comfortable and the handler is proficient it can be taken out on the road. But remember, choose somewhere quiet to begin with.

Long-line Leads

Long-line leads are generally used to teach a dog a recall cue, which is obviously important and should

Using a double-clip lead with a harness means a dog is in a good balance and the handler can manipulate their movements more easily. (Photo: Millie, courtesy of Tommy Taylor)

Long-line leads are a versatile training aid and can be used to teach a number of different training cues. (Photo: Millie and Caroline)

form part of any dog's general training. However, I include them here because they allow a fearful dog, which cannot be let off its leash, more freedom whilst the handler stays in control. They also prove invaluable when beginning to train a dog to turn and respond to the 'come away' cue (*see* 'Come Away' in Chapter 10) when working with triggers in set-ups and controlled spaces. The length of these lines varies but, for the training that is covered in the book and greater control, it's better to stick to one that is no longer than 5m (16ft).

Long-line leads look like an elongated dog lead, with a clip at one end and a handle at the other. They shouldn't be mistaken for a retractable lead, which doesn't offer a good level of control and can jar the dog's neck when being wound in. Long-line leads are usually made of fabric and come in various styles and weights. Lighter weight ones obviously suit smaller dogs and the heavier ones are better for larger breeds.

Long-line leads can be attached to either of the connection points on a harness but, to prevent the dog tripping up over it, I prefer to use the back connector. They can take a bit of getting used to and it's common to let too much length out, which can get caught around objects or tangled up around the feet and paws. Thus, the trainer will need to practise their handling skills in a safe, open space. Once mastered, they can be used in the same way as a regular lead and the dog should be able to walk loosely when one is attached as well as be taught how to slow down and stop when the handler uses the line to apply the brakes (*see* box).

Using a Long-line Lead

1. After unravelling the line it should be gathered up to form a loop in one hand.
2. After attaching the clip to the back connector of the harness, one hand should hold the line closer to the dog, while the other holds on to the handle along with the rest of the looped line.
3. The hand closest to the dog is the one that takes care of the slack, allowing the line to run through it when more freedom is required and gripping it to slow down or stop the dog when necessary.
4. The hand with the loops is the one that controls the amount of line that is released and also gathers in the length of the line to shorten it again.
5. Using both hands in this way provides a safer contact and also prevents any harsh pulling which might startle the dog as well as cause them discomfort.

House-lines

House-lines are one of my favourite pieces of equipment as they help to manipulate a dog's movements quickly and easily in a non-confrontational way. A house-line is basically a lightweight, thin, narrow house lead, usually around 2.5m (8ft) in length. It doesn't have a handle or other bulky parts and is therefore suitable to be attached to a collar and can be left to trail on behind a dog when they are in the house. Because of its design it is unlikely to get caught up, but as a safety measure they should only be used when the dog is under supervision. They are identical to a puppy-line in design and work in the same way. That is to say they can be used in the house to control a dog's movements and manoeuvre them safely without the need to make any direct physical contact, or grab hold of a collar, which can inadvertently issue a threat. They also help to back up a verbal cue, which aids training for all dogs.

Provided that aggression does not form part of the problem, a house-line can be useful for dogs that are anxious when visitors call. In those circumstances, it can be the sudden movement of the visitor as they get up to leave that triggers fear. Having a house-line means the dog can be calmly led away before the visitor moves, helping to prevent distress (*see* 'Meeting Visitors in the Home' in Chapter 10).

Baby Gates

A baby gate is a safety aid, especially useful when there are dogs and children in the house. However, as a training resource, they control a dog's movements, can help to teach a wait cue, and prevent shadowing, which can help to habituate a dog to periods of time alone. They are also an essential item for implementing in-view departures, which form part of the treatment protocols for dogs with separation anxiety issues, discussed in one of the case studies in Chapter 11.

Comfort Mats

A mat (or blanket) that is comfortable, warm and inviting isn't usually considered a training aid although, because a significant part of helping a nervous dog is fostering positive emotions and facilitating a calmer state, I usually advise owners to teach a dog to relax on a mat (*see* 'Relax on a Mat' in the training guides in Chapter 10).

A comfort mat works in much the same way as a comfort blanket does for helping a child sleep or feel more secure. Like the tone in Pavlov's experiments, the mat is initially meaningless but when paired with the feeling of being comforted and relaxed, it can take on a much more meaningful quality and induces a calmer internal state.

Comfort mats can help induce relaxation. (Photo: Ghost, courtesy of Ruth Egan-Linnecar)

A comfort mat can be extremely useful for dogs with separation anxiety or for helping dogs stay calm during situational events such as fireworks and thunderstorms. Additionally, they can be used outside the home to help mitigate the stress of car travel or for taking along to the vets where the dog can lie on it whilst being examined. Therefore, when choosing a mat, make sure it can be rolled up or folded to make it easier to carry. Artificial fleece blankets that have non-slip and water-repellent properties, like the ones used in veterinary hospitals, are ideal.

Other Useful Training Accessories

Training treat pouch

Having somewhere to store food rewards is a good idea. A pouch or bag that is easily accessible is much easier than fumbling about in a pocket. I recommend looking for something that is washable with compartments to store other items like keys, a toy, poop bags, hand-sanitizer and a phone. My personal preference is along the bum-bag design as I find them easy to access and they can be worn inside and outside the home.

Puzzle feeders and food-dispensing toys

Problem solving helps a dog exert some control within their environment, redirects mental energy and can be a

Puzzle feeders can be useful aids when working with dogs that have separation-related issues. (Photo: Rosie, courtesy of Rachel Clark)

Resources that issue a message can help to alert other people that a nervous dog requires some space. (Photo: Summer, courtesy of Ruth Egan-Linnecar)

useful distraction. Therefore these can be valuable as part of a treatment plan. There is a vast array of different kinds available but choosing the ones that are best suited to your dog's preferences makes sense. Some dogs can destroy a toy within seconds so they might require a more robust design and dogs with high levels of frustration shouldn't be given a puzzle feeder that is complicated to use.

Cameras and remote-activated food dispensers

These devices can be a useful addition to a separation anxiety treatment plan. Technology is moving at a fast pace and there is some sophisticated software available to view the dog's behaviour remotely in real time. Behaviour counsellors with a specialist interest in separation anxiety can provide support and advice about the best programmes to use and will often link in to the same application so they can be part of the live feed.

Electronic food dispensers can be set to deliver timed treats or be controlled by an owner via a remote-control device. Some even have an in-built camera facility. However, because some dogs startle at the noise of the food being delivered, it is important to desensitize them to the sound beforehand.

The Yellow Dog Project resources

This is a registered charity that aims to create awareness and educate other dog owners and the wider public that some dogs require space. Yellow ribbons attached to leads and collars, tabards and leads displaying the clear message 'I Need Space' or 'Nervous Dog' are designed to encourage people to recall their dog or move out of the way.

Developing And Practising Core Training Skills

In order to carry out some of the recommended training techniques it helps to have some basic dog-training skills and for that I recommend owners to refer to a good dog-training manual, watch video recordings of positive reinforcement dog trainers or, better still, get some face-to-face help from a suitably qualified trainer. Central to good training is timing and being consistent prevents confusion. One simple exercise that can help is bouncing a tennis ball on the ground and using your verbal marker (for example 'Yes' or 'Good') the moment it hits the floor.

Like most practical skills, getting some hands-on practice will be a necessity in order to make progress. There are a couple of core techniques that are worth working on. One is 'luring', which doesn't require too much technical skill but is really beneficial for communicating to a dog where you want to position them. The other is 'shaping', which is essentially the process of breaking down a more difficult behaviour into smaller steps.

Luring

Luring involves guiding a dog by holding a small treat right in front of their nose. In this way they can be steered to the desired position. Once there, we let them have the food reward. This method is used for basic training techniques such as the 'down' and 'sit' cue, although I have included it here because of its usefulness in teaching a dog to target and settle on a mat. I also find it useful for teaching a dog to go behind your legs as a way to shield them. Importantly, a lure should never be used to move or dislodge a frightened dog out from somewhere they feel safe or to force them into a situation they are clearly uncomfortable about. This is because a dog may experience some emotional conflict and follow the food yet, at the same time, may feel vulnerable and exposed. Approach-avoidance conflict and a heightened startle response could lead to redirected aggression. Lures should be faded out as soon as possible, transitioning first to a hand movement together with a verbal cue and then (unless the dog is deaf) a verbal cue can be used alone. But remember, lures shouldn't be used in counter-conditioning because, in luring, the food comes first and that isn't the order of things for that technique.

Shaping

Shaping involves rewarding small incremental steps towards the desired goal. It's a bit like the hot and cold game. The dog receives a verbal marker (or a click) and a reward when making moves in the right direction. By way of explanation, let's imagine that the desired outcome is for a dog to relax. To help with that, we would shape a relaxed body posture. To begin with, whenever the dog lies down, we would mark and reward them. Then each time they lie down we'd be looking for a slightly more relaxed posture like tucking in the back feet and reward that, graduating slowly to a hip roll and so on. These small approximations continue until they finally reach the end goal of taking on a relaxed posture, at which time we can begin to use a consistent cue such as 'Relax'. Of course we can begin the process by capturing and we might even use some luring to get a dog from a sit to a down position in the earlier stages of training.

Desensitization and Counter-conditioning

The concept of counter-conditioning (CC) has already been discussed but it can also be combined with systematic desensitization (DS). When used together they are effective in treating a range of fear-related problems and are central to almost all behaviour modification plans, so being able to understand how they work is critical.

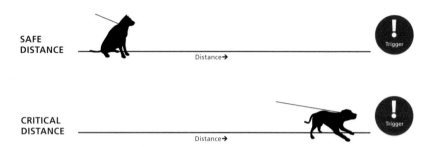

Fig. 8.1. Setting critical distances is an important factor when beginning DS and CC training.

A dog being desensitized and counter-conditioned to lorries. The distance and the use of barriers help to reduce the intensity. (Photo: Millie and Caroline)

For dogs that are highly reactive to other dogs, for safety, DS and CC may need to begin with manikins. From afar they can look realistic. (Photo: Millie and Caroline)

DS involves gradually exposing the dog to the fearful stimulus but at a rate and intensity that is insufficient to cause the specific behavioural response (fear) to occur. For some situations this involves setting a comfortable distance between the dog and whatever it is they are frightened of. We refer to this as the 'critical distance' (Fig 8.1.). Gradually the intensity, time or proximity of the stimulus is increased as the dog remains calm and unreactive at each stage. Once the dog ceases to react to the stimulus in any form, DS is complete. For DS to work effectively the dog must be relaxed and each stage must be delivered at increments that they are able to cope with. For this reason it is better if the training takes place in a controlled environment. Let the dog dictate the pace. Going too fast at a level that provokes the fearful response is detrimental and could result in flooding. It can be a slow, painstaking process but is well worth the effort.

DS and CC can be used successfully for almost any fear-related problem but are perhaps best known for treating dogs that have a fear of noises, most commonly fireworks. In that circumstance, recordings of the sound effects would be played very quietly in the background. DS alone can only get the dog from a scared to a neutral state so the positive feelings are down to CC. Therefore, whilst the dog is being desensitized, they should be engaged in doing something they find pleasurable.

When recreating a scenario, the effect has to be realistic. In the case of sound, it must represent the noise accurately. That means using good-quality recordings, played through good-quality speakers. Or when desensitizing a dog to strangers, 'stooges', rather than people the dog knows, must be used. It would also be counterproductive to work on desensitization if at any time the fearful stimulus was going to occur at full intensity. Therefore, training should commence well in advance of the frightening event taking place. For example, for dogs with firework fears, training shouldn't take place bang in the middle (pun intended) of firework season.

Suitable Training Strategies

Counter-conditioning and desensitization techniques modify behaviour and these are the mainstays of treatment for almost all fear-related problems. However, it's important to have a number of other tried and tested training strategies to call upon. While each dog is an individual, and the choice of training should be driven by their particular behavioural needs and requirements, it's highly likely that there will be some shared prerequisites. Based on that, I have narrowed the training down to include some of my favourites (Table 8.1) and you'll see how they fit into a real-life situation once you reach the case studies in Chapter 11. But don't forget there are many more that can work well so do check out the recommended reading list and follow up on some of the trainers I have mentioned to get more great ideas.

Table 8.1. Suggested training techniques to include in a behaviour modification plan. (Full step-by-step training guides can be found in Chapter 10.)

Behaviour Adjustment Training (BAT)

Another training technique worth mentioning is something called Behaviour Adjustment Training (BAT). This technique was developed by Grisha Stewart, a professional dog trainer and author based in Oregon, USA.

BAT is a positive reinforcement training method that draws on systematic desensitization techniques, marking behaviours (verbal cue or clicker), negative reinforcement and close observations of a dog's body language to guide the training. Similar to DS and CC techniques, BAT uses created situations to work at a controlled distance from the trigger. The dog is under control on a 5m (16ft) long-line so they have more freedom. With BAT, the dog is placed at a distance from the scary thing where they are comfortable but might display a very mild, low-grade stress response such as sniffing the ground, blinking or looking at the trigger and then looking away. This very subtle but contained behaviour is marked and then rewarded in two ways. One is by giving them the freedom to move away from the trigger themselves or the trainer takes the cues from their body language, for example if they become more aroused, and guides them to safer ground (those are the negative reinforcement elements). The second reinforcer is then given in the form of a food treat (or whatever else the dog finds rewarding). BAT shouldn't entail putting them under pressure to stay until they are forced to exhibit more profound signs of distress. As Grisha emphasizes, 'If you are getting complete avoidance of the trigger, you're doing something wrong.'

What I like about this technique is that it allows the dog and the handler to have a conversation about whether the dog wants to proceed or not and responding to what the dog is saying builds their trust in the handler. At the same time, BAT can help desensitize the dog to the

Table 8.1. Suggested training techniques to include in a behaviour modification plan. (Full step-by-step training guides can be found in Chapter 10.)

Training Technique	Practical Application/Benefits
Relax on a Mat	• Relaxation is a requirement for DS and CC • Can be generalized to different locations, for example helps with crate training, vet visits
Emergency U-turn	• Helps to get out of a situation quickly • Can be used when implementing Behaviour Adjustment Training (BAT) techniques
Come Away	• Useful when working with triggers in controlled situations • Can be used when implementing BAT
Hand touch training	• Manipulates the dog's movements with ease • Helps with focus and control • Useful distraction technique
Watch Me	• Helps with focus and control • Conditions frustration tolerance • Cue for a dog to look at the handler
What's That?	• Helps with focus and control • Cue for the dog to look at, or acknowledge, the frightening stimulus allowing the handler to read their level of concern
Settle or calm cue	• Can help to change emotions and induce a calmer state

fearful stimulus with the aim that they can move closer to the trigger, knowing they are in control of the pace. This technique can eventually be taken from set-up situations and used in real-life conditions.

I do have a few concerns though. This training requires a solid knowledge of canine body language and knowing when to retreat is crucial. If in doubt, help from a professional who is familiar with the technique is the best policy.

Play and Pattern Games

Some form of playful activity features in all my behaviour plans. Play heightens natural feel-good neurotransmitters but can also enhance certain aspects of a training plan. Giving the dog something else to focus on can outweigh what is going on around them and once they are caught up in the game, triggers can be introduced into the environment which can help when working on a programme of desensitization and counter-conditioning.

There's also some evidence that play enhances learning. One fairly recent study suggested that playful activities post-learning improved dogs' training performance (Affenzeller *et al.*, 2016). Hence, ending a training session with fun and games could help cement what has been taught.

Pattern games were first popularized by Leslie McDevitt, a certified dog behaviourist and author based in the USA. These are a series of different games that provide a dog with a predictable format. This concept is described in greater detail in the training guides in Chapter 10, along with one or two games to try out. Basically, pattern games follow a clear structure and once a dog learns the rules of the game they begin to predict what comes next, which increases their sense of security.

From a practical point of view, choosing pattern games that add movement can be useful in keeping a dog on

BAT Training: (a) A low-grade stress signal in response to a stranger. (Photo: Barney, courtesy of Allen Redfearn)

BAT Training: (b) Being guided safely back to the trainer (and rewarded). (Photo: Barney, courtesy of Allen Redfearn)

Playing with a dog at the end of a training session can help to cement learning and is a reward for their hard work and concentration. (Photo: Millie and Caroline, courtesy of Tommy Taylor)

the go – essential if you need to get them out of trouble quickly. Also, movement can help a dog feel more in control and less threatened. Asking a frightened dog to focus and be still when they are restrained on a lead is probably what drives some to lunge and bark. After all, what else can they do? That's why pattern games and other training methods that incorporate movement away from the target are often more successful.

Life Rewards

Very often, when our dog has a behaviour problem we are concerned with trying to stop the dog from performing that behaviour. 'Life reward' training is concerned with rewarding behaviours we do want. Life rewards can become part of a dog owner's normal routine in the same way as capturing.

A life reward is anything that a dog wants in their daily life. It could be food, play or access to something they want, like attention or off-lead exercise but, before we give it to them, we politely ask them to do something for us. It can be anything in their repertoire of taught behaviours such as sit, paw, or a hand target touch – nothing too demanding. Think of it as being a way of saying please. If they don't respond immediately, we just calmly ask again. The aim of this exercise is to encourage a dog to always turn to us for direction, teaching them that it is important and valuable to listen. Getting them into this habit means we always have a window of opportunity to guide and direct them in a difficult situation. Unpredictability can provoke anxiety and so life reward training can also help by building consistency into a dog's world.

The Owner's Impact On Dog Behaviour

As we have already established, dogs are very perceptive. They can detect our changing emotions through the odours we emit and are masters at reading body language, even ours. Therefore we should always be mindful of the impact we can have on their behaviour. When a dog owner projects feelings of calmness and confidence, dogs tend to feel safer. Conversely, when owners are anxious there is a tendency for the dog to look to their environment for signs of danger – there must be some reason that the owner is feeling (and smelling) anxious! So before training a dog or taking them out, it really helps if you feel mentally prepared too.

Here are some simple tactics that might help:

- Learn some calming techniques. Simple deep-breathing exercises can help.
- Practise and improve your dog-handling techniques at home to gain confidence.
- Think about practical ways to manage the environment to reduce your own and your dog's anxiety.
- Develop a closer relationship with your dog by engaging in fun activities together.
- If going out on walks in uncontrolled environments proves stressful, and is damaging to your relationship, stop going. Hire a private dog-walking field and concentrate on other enrichment activities at home whilst taking time out to work on the problem.
- Play pattern games and learn how to make the most of training opportunities on walks.

- Take up yoga, meditation and exercise in green spaces.
- Don't suffer alone. Join a support group or see a human counsellor.
- Seek professional help from a clinical animal behaviourist and work on training techniques with a suitably qualified trainer.

Key Take Home Points

- Health and safety should be a priority to safeguard members of the public and the dog.
- Get the right equipment and practise some core dog-training skills in quiet settings with no distractions.
- Desensitization and counter-conditioning are effective in the treatment of fear-related problems but require careful planning and patience.
- Training techniques that fulfil the dog's needs and have a practical element should be incorporated into a behaviour treatment plan.
- A programme of training provides a dog with familiar routines that can have a calming effect.
- Play and pattern games can augment learning.
- Our emotions can transfer to the dog, so being mentally prepared for handling and training is important.

CHAPTER 9

The Benefits of Complementary and Integrated Treatments

Formulating a targeted behaviour plan calls for a holistic approach. In other words, rather than focusing solely on the problematic behaviour, it helps to look at the dog as a whole. Taking this line allows the behaviourist to consider additional treatments rather than concentrating on the training techniques alone. In the world of animal behaviour counselling we usually refer to these add-ons as adjuncts.

Drawing from human medicine, we know how useful certain complementary therapies can be for mental (and physical) health issues and evidence is pointing us in the same direction when addressing animal health problems. Complementary therapies that can be included as part of a behaviour plan range from the more typical dietary supplements to mind-body therapies that are suited to dogs, such as groundwork and mental enrichment (Table 9.1). Whilst many of these treatments can easily be implemented at home, and are available without a prescription, in the main, complementary therapies should only operate alongside conventional treatment and should not replace it. Also, like clinical animal behaviourists, anyone offering a particular therapy ought to do so with permission from the owner's veterinary surgeon. In this chapter I introduce a handful of treatments that might prove useful for some dogs.

Table 9.1. Examples of some of the complementary treatments that can be used alongside a behaviour modification plan.

Complementary Behavioural Therapy	Examples of Actual (and Potential) Benefits
Acupuncture (strictly a veterinary procedure)	• Neurotransmitter release • Normalizing effects on the autonomic nervous system • Pain-killing properties can help relieve pain-induced stress
Aromatherapy	• Olfactory stimulation to enhance the release of neurotransmitters
Dietary supplements	• Influence neurotransmitters • Antioxidant and neuro-protection

OPPOSITE: Ghost, courtesy of Ruth Egan-Linnecar.

Complementary Behavioural Therapy	Examples of Actual (and Potential) Benefits
Groundwork	• Release of neurotransmitters • Mentally stimulating • Improves physical and emotional balance
Herbalism	• Various effects dependent on plants selected
Homeopathy	• Various effects dependent on remedy prescribed
Mental enrichment	• Release of neurotransmitters • Mentally stimulating
Music	• Certain genres induce relaxation
Pheromone therapy (DAP)	• Induces calmness
Touch therapy	• Release of neurotransmitters • Promotes relaxation

Dietary Supplements

The most common forms of therapy that owners turn to, and vets will dispense as a basic first-line treatment for fear-related behaviours, are non-prescription calming supplements. These are added to the diet, usually in a tablet, capsule or powdered form. Preparations contain selected ingredients that have been recognized for their calming or mood-lifting properties (Table 9.2). There still isn't an abundance of scientific evidence available but there are a great many positive reports coming back from owners who have used them on their dogs.

I usually include some form of dietary supplement in my treatment plans, some of which I have included here. However, on their own, they are unlikely to cure a dog suffering from significant fear and anxiety. Nothing replaces behaviour modification. My general advice is to look at the labels, see what they contain and do your own research. Remember to be cautious. Certain over-the-counter treatments, such as St John's Wort (*Hypericum perforatum*), used for human anxiety, can interact with other medication, which can pose a serious risk to the dog. As always, liaise with your veterinary surgeon.

Alpha-caseozepine

Alpha-caseozepine is a supplement that a number of vets supply for generalized and situational anxiety. Like many other products, this falls under a category described as a nutraceutical. These are non-prescription food supplements, with purported medicinal or health benefits. However, the food laws that govern them forbid the manufacturers from making medical claims.

Alpha-caseozepine is a natural ingredient derived from casein, a protein found in mammalian milk. If you have ever witnessed mammals relaxing after breastfeeding it's not hard to imagine why researchers were keen to determine if this protein could be used in a therapeutic way. Having found that it had a similar structure to the neurotransmitter GABA, it was produced in a dried formula and is available in capsule form. It can also be found as an ingredient in certain dog food preparations.

L-Tryptophan

L-Tryptophan (tryptophan) features high on the list of ingredients in many anti-anxiety supplements and so is worth some mention here. Tryptophan is an amino-acid (a simple molecule that forms proteins) found in meat and other protein-containing foods. One of its properties is to help in the formation of serotonin, the neurotransmitter known for its effect on well-being. Constant and regular release of cortisol inhibits serotonin production, so using natural supplements that help increase it would be useful for stressed dogs.

Low concentrations of tryptophan have been associated with insomnia, anxiety and depression in humans and one study in dogs suggested that tryptophan

Table 9.2. A selection of dietary substances used for their behavioural effects.

Dietary Substance	Behavioural Effects
Alpha-caseozepine	• A protein found in mammalian milk. Similar in composition to GABA
Carotenoids	• Anti-oxidant and neuro-protective properties
Essential fatty acids and long-chain polyunsaturated fatty acids (PUFA) for example omega-3	• Neuro-protection • Play a key role in early brain development • Anti-oxidant properties
Glutamate	• A brain energy source • Aids communication between neurons
L-Tryptophan	• Precursor to serotonin
Probiotics	• Healthy gut bacteria may aid digestion and in turn help alleviate some forms of anxiety
Selenium (mineral)	• A trace element with neuro-protective abilities
Vitamin B6	• Helps in the production of serotonin
Vitamins C and E	• Neuro-protective and anti-oxidant properties

supplementation of a low-protein diet may be helpful in reducing territorial aggression. To be effective, tryptophan needs to cross the blood-brain barrier and that can be hampered by a number of complex factors. Therefore there is no guarantee that sufficient levels will make it to the brain. That said, food scientist and dog behaviourist Val Strong has developed a serotonin-enhancing complete dog food that is designed to overcome some of these problems. Feeding trials and studies have been very promising and it's definitely one that I will be following with great interest.

Neuro-protective Supplements

There has been a growing interest in using certain food components to help guard against, and support, canine cognitive dysfunction (CCD). Diets and supplements have been formulated containing compounds that help enhance brain energy and protect the neurons. The idea is that by keeping the signalling systems intact, memory and cognition remain functional.

There are a number of products on the market and because CCD can lead to anxiety and other behaviour changes, it's worth chatting to a veterinarian about including them in the diet of an elderly dog. It should be noted that impaired blood flow to the brain can also be implicated in CCD and veterinary treatment for that is available.

Probiotics

Probiotics are live microorganisms that are often described as friendly bacteria. These are said to aid digestion due to their ability to help maintain a healthy gut balance. More recently there is some suggestion that manipulation of the gut microbiota (the good bacteria that aid digestion) can influence behaviour and a study, yet to be published, by the Purina Institute showed that a specific microbiota (*Bifidobacterium longum*) has anxiety-reducing effects on anxious dogs when compared with dogs fed a placebo diet.

Unfortunately, supplements containing that specific microbiota don't seem to be widely available in the UK (at the time of writing) but probiotics are generally very safe so trialling them in the diet (for at least eight weeks), in tandem with veterinary support, may be worthwhile. It should however be noted that strains added to many calming supplements have not necessarily been identified to have behavioural effects. Nonetheless they may still aid digestive disturbances and we know that stress can affect the gut and vice-versa, so they may help.

Plants and Herbs

Herbalism involves using parts of a plant for their medicinal properties. This practice stretches back thousands of years and even today the World Health Organization (WHO) estimate that 70 per cent of the world's population use botanical medicine. Herbs and plant extracts are key ingredients in a number of pharmaceutical preparations used for both human and animal health and here in the UK the British Association of Veterinary Herbalists (BAVH) has a register of qualified specialist practitioners who use herbal treatments, often alongside conventional veterinary therapies.

Some of the herbs used in many non-prescription calming supplements include lemon balm extract, said to alleviate agitation, marigold, calendula, chamomile, passion flower (*Passiflora incarnata*), skullcap and valerian, all chosen for their calmative properties. However, because of the toxic nature of certain plants, and the potential for some to interact with conventional medication, I would recommend only using them as part of a veterinary-endorsed preparation or seeking help from a veterinary herbalist.

Aromatherapy

Aromatherapy uses plant extracts to produce aromatic essential oils that promote feelings of well-being. Although this therapy, and the feedback about its effects, remains largely in the realm of human health, there is some evidence that it might have a place in canine behaviour.

In one study, shelter dogs exposed to lavender and chamomile oil were shown to spend more time resting and less time moving around and barking (Graham *et al.*, 2005).

Lavender was also used in a study to evaluate its efficacy as a treatment for travel-induced excitement and during the experimental period the dogs spent significantly more time resting and less time moving around the car and vocalizing (Wells, 2006). Other aromas chosen for their calming properties and commercially available in sprays and diffusers include combinations of valerian oil, vetiver, sweet basil, and clary sage essential oils.

Some essential oils can be dangerous if ingested. Tea tree oil in particular is extremely toxic to dogs. Also, diffusers and warmers can be overpowering and what might be pleasant or interesting to one dog might be extremely unpleasant to another. For this reason I would never rub the oils into the dog's coat or skin and instead recommend using scent-infused cloths to introduce the dog to the smell. These can be placed in the dog's environment to give them the freedom to say no, by moving away, or to investigate further. In this way it is possible to assess their preferences.

Self-selection of non-toxic plants and herbs (for example chamomile, clary sage, lavender, valerian) in the garden is another, perhaps safer, method of introduction. Pots or beds, where the dog walks and can brush against, just below nose height, create a sensory experience. This arrangement has proved particularly beneficial for dogs in shelters and can offer additional enrichment for extremely reactive or traumatized dogs that are having some time out from walks whilst they undergo rehabilitation training.

Pheromone Therapy

The discovery that the naturally occurring dog appeasing pheromone (DAP) could be delivered through a synthetic equivalent gave us an additional complementary treatment for canine anxiety. There have been numerous studies citing the effectiveness of DAP, including those that have shown the benefits of using it to help dogs adapt to unfamiliar environments. For this reason, as well as its calming effects, it is widely used in veterinary clinics, grooming salons, boarding kennels and shelters. DAP can be delivered through infused collars, sprays and diffusers. As with other complementary treatments, it is designed for use in combination with other techniques and, other than mild cases, is unlikely to work as a standalone treatment.

A bandana with synthetic versions of the dog appeasing pheromone sprayed on it may help to induce calmness. (Photo: Bella, courtesy of Sadie Fox)

Touch and Pressure

The use of pressure to calm animals has been explored, although this has primarily focused on livestock species. Nonetheless, from this work, and studies carried out in humans, it does appear that pressure on soft tissue can help to reduce anxiety. Although the mechanisms are not fully understood it is thought that certain pressure points prompt the release of dopamine, serotonin and natural opioids (pain-killing chemicals). Touch therapy at its most basic can include petting and stroking a dog, which most of us perform on our dogs almost instinctively. On the whole most dogs respond positively although it's important to remember that some could find being touched extremely stressful.

Perhaps the touch therapy that has attracted the most interest is the Tellington Touch (TTouch) method. This technique was developed by Linda Tellington Jones back

The ear slide is a TTouch technique, useful for inducing calmness. Hold the ear flap horizontally between the fingers and thumb and gently stroke it. Work from the top of the ear (closest to the head) down to the tip. (Photo: Millie and Caroline)

in the 1970s when she began using non-threatening, intentional touch techniques and groundwork as part of her training system for horses. This approach worked well in relaxing the horses and improved their focus, balance and movement. Some years later the method was adapted and TTouch is now practised throughout the world to help handle, train and rehabilitate many animal species.

There are a number of different touches but, rather than deep massage, the technique generally calls for a very light, gentle movement of the skin through specialized circular touches, lifts and slides. Specially trained practitioners can carry out treatments that suit the individual case, although attending a workshop is an extremely useful way of learning some of the techniques to carry out on your own dog.

Compression Shirts and Body Wraps

Compression shirts apply gentle, constant pressure around the dog's torso and, in a similar way to swaddling an infant or hugging someone when they are distressed, it is believed that this has a calming effect. Body wraps are essentially wide, elasticated bandages and these work in a similar way although, when used as part of the TTouch method, they also increase body awareness. As with any new piece of equipment, I advise that a dog undergoes some desensitization training beforehand because getting them on might be stressful.

Compression shirts that exert pressure around the torso can help some dogs but require a careful approach when being fitted. (Photo: Rufus, courtesy of Amy Clark)

After fitting, it's important to observe the dog for signs of anxiety. Some dogs become quiet and less responsive which can be interpreted as the dog calming down when in fact, they feel so overwhelmed and inhibited by them, they shut down altogether. For this reason caution should be exercised.

Opinion as to whether they work is divided and the data is limited but one study, printed in the *Journal of Veterinary Science*, did seem to suggest that using a Thundershirt (a type of anxiety shirt) may help to reduce anxiety in dogs and so, with the necessary care, they may be worth considering as an adjunct to a behaviour modification plan.

Music and Sound

The most obvious use of music in a behaviour plan tends to be as a method of masking frightening sounds.

However, several different types of music have been tested in dogs for their ability to relax and calm. Classical music appears to be the genre most successful in inducing relaxation and many rescue shelters report that playing relaxing classical music in the background seems to help. Other sounds that have been shown to help include people talking and one recent study found that listening to a male voice reading an audiobook was even more successful in inducing relaxation than music. Perhaps, unsurprisingly, rock and heavy metal music were found to increase barking, vocalizing and standing behaviours.

Mental Enrichment

You might have already guessed by now but I am a great advocate of mental enrichment. Without exception, it's in all my plans. Because all dogs know how to use their sense of smell, anything that gets them sniffing is usually

Containers made of safe materials can be filled with food and on a good day, placed outside so the dog has to physically and mentally work at retrieving the food. (Photo: Millie)

Enriched feeding can be a mental challenge and prolonged chewing and licking can reduce stress. (Photo: Missie, courtesy of Julia Clark)

Incorporating Mental Enrichment into a Dog's Daily Routine

- Ditch the bowl and scatter-feed dried kibble.
- Sprinkle small treats on the lawn or in a pile of leaves.
- Use snuffle mats to hide food and treats.
- Play search and find games by hiding food and toys around the house and garden.
- On walks, throw a toy or a treat into the shrubs for the dog to find.
- Using a phrase such as 'Go find' can be useful because this can be used to put the behaviour on cue.

Seek and find games on walks gets a dog working and using their mind. (Photo: Millie and Caroline, courtesy of Tommy Taylor)

a winner. Using the nose and foraging is inherently reinforcing. It has been shown that a dog's pulse rate lowers when they are given the opportunity to sniff (so let them sniff on walks) and the higher the sniffing intensity the lower the pulse rate becomes. When the head is down a dog is less likely to be vigilant and it's incompatible with scanning the environment so it serves a useful function in more ways than one.

Mental enrichment can start with meal times. Dogs were designed to work to get their food. This normal activity took up a large part of their time budget and energy. Consequently they had less time to display inappropriate behaviours and kept physically fit. With domesticity, this activity has been eroded. For most dogs, meal times are over in a matter of seconds. This can lead to boredom and a reservoir of energy that needs to be expended. For high-energy breeds, interactive feeding provides an outlet for their mental and physical energy. For older dogs it can be a way of keeping the joints moving and the brain active, preventing cognitive decline. It's extremely beneficial for anxious dogs too as it redirects all their nervous energy into a mentally enriching task, whilst at the same time it floods the system with feel-good hormones.

Groundwork and Exercise

Groundwork is another aspect of the TTouch method. This involves leading a dog through what is known as a 'confidence course'. The leading exercises incorporate slow, deliberate movements over simple equipment such as ramps, poles and wobble boards that aim to improve their balance and encourages them to explore and problem solve in more measured, mindful way. This can be incredibly beneficial for dogs that find it difficult to switch off.

With some imagination it is possible to design something similar at home and you can mix things up with treats along the way to help guide a dog through and over the obstacles. Laying poles on the ground, setting up weaving posts as well as creating different surfaces using mats or bark chippings to walk over can easily be arranged. This kind of mental and physical agility course can help to build a dog's confidence and focuses their attention on performing a task in their own time and without any pressure.

With imagination it's possible to set up your own groundwork. (Photo: Millie and Caroline)

Sharing fun activities with your dog enhances dog-owner bonds. (Photo: Oscar, courtesy of Charlotte Wood, York Mantrailing)

Animal Centred Education (ACE) is the brainchild of Sarah Fisher, a TTouch practitioner, who has built on the groundwork principles to develop a structured, hands-off approach that allows dogs to engage in a sensory experience without having to deal with human touch. ACE has a list of practitioners and also host practical workshops for anyone who wishes to learn some of the techniques to benefit their own dog.

Physical exercise has been promoted in human healthcare because of its mental health benefits and this applies to animals too. Groundwork and pattern games both incorporate movement. However, there are many other activities to choose from that suit different dogs and their owners. Agility, flyball, CaniCross (a sport where owners and dogs take part in cross-country running) and Mantrailing (where dogs follow a scent to find a 'missing' person) are just some of the activities available although just being in the outdoors and going

Expending energy in a fun way (flyball) induces the release of feel-good neurotransmitters. (Photo: Harvey, courtesy of Michelle Porteus)

out for a regular walk is most beneficial. Expending energy helps to flood the system with lots of feel-good hormones, relieves tension and improves the dog's (and our) quality of sleep. Finding the right environment for some reactive dogs can be tricky although, in the UK, there are a network of dog parks which are available for private hire and this allows a dog to run free, unhindered.

Acupuncture

Acupuncture evolved from traditional Chinese medicine and has been practised for thousands of years. The technique involves piercing the skin with specially adapted fine needles that stimulate the nervous system. When carried out on animals it is considered a veterinary treatment and can therefore only be carried out by a qualified veterinarian who has received specialist training.

Scientific research into acupuncture is extensive and there is now greater recognition and acceptance of it within the scientific community. Traditionally, it was more commonly used for pain relief (brought about by natural pain-killing, opioid responses). However, deeper understanding has revealed the positive effects it has on mental and physical health and the Yin and Yang balance can now be explained with links to the parasympathetic and sympathetic nervous system. Typically, acupuncture is used when pain and inflammation are thought to be provoking a behaviour response but perhaps we should consider its beneficial properties in restoring emotional equilibrium.

Homeopathy

Like acupuncture, homeopathy can only be practised by a veterinary surgeon and The British Association of Homeopathic Veterinary Surgeons has a list of accredited practitioners. The therapeutics of homeopathy are based on the philosophy of 'Let like treat like' and there are a range of treatments available for various emotional issues in animals. However, this is one area of veterinary medicine where there is still some division and because scientific evidence is currently lacking, the Royal College of Veterinary Surgeons have deemed it a complementary therapy and not a standalone treatment.

Key Take Home Points

- A holistic approach helps to create a more balanced treatment plan.
- Complementary therapies can be useful adjuncts to a behaviour modification plan.
- Scientific research on certain complementary therapies can be limited and some can be harmful, so care must be exercised. If in doubt speak to a veterinarian.
- Mentally enriching activities and/or physical exercise should always be integrated into a behaviour modification plan.

10

Training Guides

In this chapter you will find a collection of training guides. Each one provides step-by-step instructions of how to teach your dog some of the recommended training that has been referred to throughout the book. However, it is not a definitive training guide. Therefore having some basic dog-training skills may be necessary and ideally your dog should already know and understand some basic dog-training cues.

I have listed some suitable dog-training books in the Further Resources section at the back of the book, and these should help. Nevertheless, it's important that you set yourself and the dog up to succeed, so do get some help and support from a suitably qualified professional if you struggle with any aspects of the training.

The Stages Of Learning

There are four basic stages of learning:

- Acquisition
- Fluency
- Generalization
- Maintenance

Acquisition is the first stage of learning. This phase encompasses the period from when the dog starts out to when they begin to improve their performance. Initially they require a lot of assistance but gradually they begin to learn without as much help. However, they are still not yet proficient and require further practice to respond with greater accuracy. During this stage the dog must be trained where there are no distractions

and where they feel the safest, which, for most dogs, is inside the house.

The next stage is fluency and this comes with practice. This stage is reached when the dog responds to the new cue immediately and requires less assistance. Now is the time to begin training in different rooms of the house and adding in a few distractions. In the garden, on a quiet day, might be a good place to progress as there will be different sights, sounds and scents. It's common for a dog to regress slightly but work should continue in each new environment until they are fluent. Only then should they be moved to a slightly more distracting setting.

Generalization comes next. Reaching this stage can take some time to achieve because the dog must be able to respond to the training in lots of different and distracting situations. For fearful dogs, this can be difficult. Gradual progress is crucial and for more demanding cases, professional help may be required.

Maintenance is the final stage of learning. This relates to the retention of knowledge, which means practising the training every now and again to make sure your dog (and you) don't forget how to perform the task accurately.

Tips for Training

- A dog must be below threshold when starting a training session. Gauge their mood state.
- If you're not in a good mood, don't train.
- Remember it's only a reward if the dog desires it.
- Use highly valued treats that a dog will work hard for and retain control of them.
- Treats should be no bigger than a pea.

OPPOSITE: Millie, courtesy of Tommy Taylor.

- For extremely good work use a highly valued reward. This is referred to as a 'jackpot'. In other words save their all-time absolute favourite treat for their best responses.
- To prevent the dog gaining weight from the extra calories, reduce their daily food ration and avoid fatty and calorific treats.
- Dogs will work harder if they are on the hungry side so always train before meals.
- Be quick with rewards. Ideally they should be given within one second of the desired action. Where this is not possible, use verbal markers (or clickers) to help bridge a gap between the behaviour and the reward.
- Short regular sessions of around three to five minutes' duration, three times a day are better than long intermittent ones. Puppies have a shorter attention span so one to two minute durations are sufficient.
- Training doesn't always have to be a formal affair. Have treats handy so that you can capture and reward behaviours anytime, anywhere.
- Be consistent and reward good behaviour abundantly.
- Ignore unwanted behaviour.
- All members of the family should follow the same procedure to avoid confusion.
- Sometimes it can help to give the dog a signal of no reward. For example, if a dog is trying another behaviour instead of the one you want, I like to use a very calm 'Not that' or 'Whoops'. This signal means try something else. When they do, and it happens to be the correct action, reward immediately. Obviously help them out if they are struggling and rethink whether you need to teach them using a different method. Like us, all dogs learn differently.
- Use a release signal at the end of a taught behaviour so the dog knows they can leave their position or stop their activity. For example, 'Free' or 'Off you go'.
- If a secure and controlled venue is going to be difficult to arrange, be inventive. For example, to work with dogs that are fearful of other dogs, try and find somewhere overlooking a veterinary car park, where dogs are on leads and are controlled. Or using a large car park at a quiet time might provide the right environment when working with dogs that are fearful of traffic.
- Make sure training is fun.
- Always end the training session on a positive note and have a play session to help embed learning.

Crate Training

Crates come in many different designs but they must be large enough for the dog to move around and stand upright comfortably. Due to a dog's social nature, the crate should not be placed in an isolated location and they must never be used for 'time out' otherwise a negative association may develop with it.

The Benefits of Crate Training

- They can be used as the dog's safe haven.
- They can be used for health and safety purposes when there are children/toddlers in the home.
- For safe car travel and transportation.
- They can help habituate a dog to being confined (for example for hospitalization purposes).

A crate should represent a safe and secure place to rest so make sure it is comfortable and inviting. However, a dog cannot be expected to be confined for extended periods, when they are hungry, in need of the toilet or require exercise. Everyone in the family must respect the crate as the dog's safe haven and children should be taught to give the dog peace and quiet when they are there.

The Training Steps

1. Introduce a dog to the crate as early as possible. If you begin when they are puppies it will be easier, but older dogs can be taught too.
2. Place it in a quiet, but not completely isolated, area and leave the door open.
3. Make the crate as comfortable as possible – it can help to place it where your dog usually sleeps.
4. Partially covering it with a blanket can help it feel more like a den.
5. Use familiar and comfortable bedding.
6. Consider using dog appeasing pheromone products on the bedding or in a diffuser close by to create a calming environment.
7. Place treats, toys or meals in the crate so that the dog is motivated to enter.
8. Never force them inside.
9. Reward a dog for entering the crate themselves.
10. Sit next to the crate, calmly and quietly, after they have had a play session or when they are tired and resting.

11. Encourage the dog to go in the crate after exercise when they might be feeling tired.
12. A comfort blanket/mat that has been used to teach a 'Relax on a Mat' can be placed inside but not if they already have a negative association with the crate. This will require more work and the comfort mat may lose its positive appeal.
13. When a dog is comfortable entering the crate voluntarily it is possible to desensitize them to relaxing inside with the door shut.
14. When they are engaged in a self-reinforcing activity (interactive feeder or a toy) close the door very briefly (for one to two seconds).
15. Open the door and praise them.
16. *Very* gradually (second by second) increase the time they are inside with the door closed but do not leave them alone.
17. If they are resting you can sit quietly close by, reading or doing something that makes you feel relaxed.
18. Once they are relaxing and not objecting to being in the crate with the door closed, leave the room very briefly but make sure you are in sight to begin with.
19. Return and open the crate door, praising and rewarding as before.
20. Gradually increase the time with in-view absences but vary the amount of time from short absences (two to three seconds) to slightly longer ones (five to eight seconds) and so on.
21. Progress to very brief out-of-view absences. A baby gate can be useful so the door to the room can remain open. This feels less isolating.

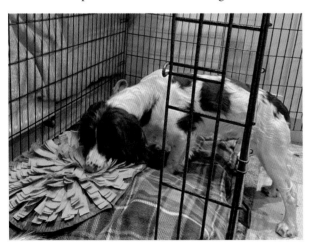

Crate training, step 7. A snuffle mat can motivate a dog to step into their crate. (Photo: Rufus, courtesy of Amy Clark)

Crate training, steps 11 and 12. Post-exercise tiredness and a comfortable blanket can encourage use of the crate. (Photo: Rufus, courtesy of Amy Clark)

22. Gradually the time can be increased.
23. Remote cameras can be used to check the dog's reactions. Make sure you can return before they show any signs of distress.

Training in this way ensures that your dog does not become frightened of being confined.

Never leave a dog to cry or become distressed. This only causes them to have negative associations with the crate and is counter-productive to training.

Muzzle Training

Why Use a Muzzle?
Muzzles are used for many different reasons including:

- Preventing injuries to others (frightened dogs can bite).
- As a method to carry out a veterinary procedure safely.
- To carry out a first-aid procedure (pain can induce aggression).
- In the UK, certain breeds of dog, identified on the dangerous dog list have to, by law, be muzzled in public places.

Choosing a Muzzle
Muzzles should be comfortable and well fitted. Basket-style muzzles allow a dog to pant, drink and receive treats through the bars. Material muzzles are not recommended

other than for very quick procedures in the veterinary environment, as they don't allow a dog to drink or pant.

The Training Steps

1. Begin by introducing a dog to the muzzle when they are calm and relaxed.
2. Assuming they haven't already formed a negative association with it, place it close by so they can see it and investigate it on their own terms.
3. If the muzzle has a clip fastener, begin clipping and unclipping it in their presence. After clipping the fastener, follow up with a reward. If they show any signs of alarm, reduce the intensity by moving further away.
4. When the dog has accepted its presence, smear the inside and outside with something tasty like creamed cheese, pâté or peanut butter (free from Xylitol which is toxic to dogs).
5. Encourage them to lick and explore the muzzle for them to gain a positive association with it.
6. Once they are happily doing this, hold the treat-laden muzzle as if it were a bowl. This helps encourage them to voluntarily place their nose inside it. Praise them continually.
7. Begin to hold the muzzle very still as if it were being offered up for them to put it over their nose. Avoid pushing it on and let them enter their nose in it in their own time.
8. You can lay the straps gently over their neck at this stage but don't attempt to fasten them yet.
9. Begin to move around so they have to physically move towards you and the tasty muzzle. This can be turned into a game with lots of praise for offering the behaviour.
10. Now add a verbal marker such as 'Yes' or 'Good' each time they put their nose inside the muzzle. Follow this up with a reward. Repeat this exercise until the dog is happily placing their nose into the muzzle.
11. At this stage, as you present the muzzle, you can add the predictive cue: 'Muzzle'. This helps a dog prepare for the muzzle being introduced and prevents any alarm.
12. Provided the dog is progressing, briefly introduce the straps and fasten the muzzle for a second or two.
13. Increase the duration that the muzzle is in place (second by second).

Muzzle training, step 4. Squirty cheese is a handy treat.

Muzzle training, step 5. Create a positive association with the muzzle.

Muzzle training, step 6. Offer the muzzle and let the dog enter of their own accord.

14. As well as smearing the muzzle with creamed cheese, treats can be passed through the bars as a reward.

It is not uncommon for a dog to try to paw at the muzzle during the early stages of training. A good tip is to keep them moving forward. Make sure praise and a reward are given when they do stop pawing in order to teach them acceptance.

As with all training, if a dog has difficulties progressing through the stages, be prepared to take a step back. They may just need a bit more time.

Harness Training

Harnesses generally tend to be more comfortable and help to control a dog without putting pressure around the sensitive structures around the neck and throat. However, fitting them on a fearful dog can be a cause of stress and requires a sensitive approach.

The Training Steps

1. Start by leaving the harness in the areas of the home where the dog spends most of their time, allowing them to see it and investigate it with their noses in their own time.
2. Provided they don't show any signs of alarm, place it somewhere close by (but not encroaching on their space) whilst they are engaged in doing something pleasant. This should help them begin to make positive associations with it.
3. After a few days, lay it somewhere with treats scattered around it so they have to get closer still, making sure they do so on their own terms.
4. Gradually, if all goes well, the harness can be lifted so that the part that goes over their head forms a loop. You or a helper can then pass a hand through the loop, offering the dog a treat. It's important not to rush this stage, as advancing the loop over the head too soon can be frightening.
5. Some dogs really don't like the feeling of someone approaching them head on. For that reason, I prefer to place myself at the side of the dog so they don't feel threatened.
6. Very gradually, the hand with the treat in it should be withdrawn so that the dog has to advance closer to the loop. Work should continue until eventually they are putting their head through it.
7. For extremely nervous dogs, make sure you have selected a harness with a neck clip so they don't have to put their head through the loop. Instead work on desensitizing them to the feel of it on their body before moving on to the next step.
8. At this stage, the harness can be briefly laid over the back of the neck, making sure that treats are still being given.
9. In between this process it's a good idea to introduce them to the sound of the clasps opening and closing. It's often this noise that can startle a dog, especially if they are noise sensitive. Begin this procedure at a comfortable distance away from them, again, whilst they are doing something pleasant. Progress to working at a closer proximity and with each click of the clasp, follow up with a treat so that the sound predicts something good is happening.
10. Once the dog is relaxed about hearing the clasps, and is comfortable with the sensation of the harness on their body, one of the clasps can be fastened. Treats should still be given in abundance.
11. Continue in this way, breaking the task into very small steps, until the harness is in situ and both clasps are fastened.
12. Now it's time to get them used to wearing the harness. Initially this should be only for a few seconds, slowly progressing to longer periods of time. Lots of praise, treats and maybe even a short game should be initiated.

Harness training, step 3. Encourage the dog to get close to the harness with treats.

Harness training, step 4. Introduce the harness lifted in the air, but don't rush to put it over the dog's head.

Harness training, step 6. Lure the dog with a treat to move their head towards and ultimately through the harness.

Harness training, step 11. Through small, sequential steps, the harness can be applied and fastened.

13. If at any time the dog shows any signs of fear or anxiety, just go back in their training to a stage they were comfortable with, and proceed more slowly.

Relax on a Mat

Having a specific mat (or blanket) to relax and chill out on is really useful for all dogs but especially so for those that are fearful and anxious. Relaxation is fundamental to desensitization and counter-conditioning protocols and, once a dog is trained, just seeing and resting on it can induce feelings of relaxation, which can offset stress and anxiety. To enhance the mat as a place to relax, you can use herbal aromas, dog appeasing pheromones or an article of your worn clothing with your scent on it.

The mat or blanket might be placed on top of an existing bed but the idea is that it can easily be taken out and relocated wherever you want it to help induce calmness and familiarity.

The Benefits

This training can be used for inducing relaxation:

- During programmes of desensitization and counter-conditioning (**DS CC**).
- When crate training, creating dens and doggy safe spaces.
- When habituating a dog to be alone.
- As part of a treatment protocol for separation anxiety disorders.
- When travelling/being transported.
- In boarding kennels, grooming parlours.
- For veterinary examinations and hospitalization.

It might take a number of weeks before you get to the end of the training but once a dog begins to understand the cue, it's surprising how quickly they learn.

The Training Steps

1. Place the mat on the floor.
2. To start with, even if the dog just looks at the mat, verbally mark the behaviour (or click) and reward.
3. When using food rewards, throw the treat a small distance away. This encourages them to move away from the mat.

4. Once the dog is beginning to understand that it's coming towards the mat that earns them the reward, start to make the training just a fraction harder by moving away from the mat.

5. Now wait until your dog places a paw on the mat. Repeat the verbal cue and reward as before.

6. Repeat a few times until you can see that your dog is consistently approaching the mat and stepping on it.

7. Now raise the criteria by waiting for two front paws to be on the mat. Don't worry if they seem to be trying lots of other different behaviours. It's common for dogs to try every trick they know to get the reward – so be patient.

8. It is human nature to want to help your dog out but try to avoid getting in the way of their learning. Looking at the mat can be useful to give them a little clue or touching the edge of it with your toe can help. But, unless your dog is really confused, wait just a few seconds for them to offer the behaviour. Waiting gives a dog the chance to work it out for themselves and, when they do, they really start to make rapid progress.

9. Once a dog is getting their front paws on the mat consistently, hold off marking the behaviour until they get three paws on the mat. Remember to always throw a treat a small distance away from the mat.

10. The idea is to shape their behaviour until all four paws are on the mat.

11. For really good progress you can give them a 'jackpot' so that your dog knows they have done a really great job.

12. Once a dog is consistently approaching the mat we can add a verbal cue such as 'Go to mat'. You might want to add a hand signal too.

13. Now, with the verbal cue, begin to drop the treat on the mat ready for the relaxation part of the training.

14. To build duration in to the training, wait a little longer before giving the marker and reward. Start with a second in time, very gradually building up the duration.

15. Outside of training, capture the behaviour whenever they voluntarily go on the mat. We really want them to know that going on the mat gets them a great reward!

16. The next stage is waiting for them to go into a down posture (or use a 'Down' if they already know the cue).

17. Once you have them targeting the mat and lying down we can shape the behaviour so that they are lying down in a more relaxed posture. For most dogs it's when the hip is relaxed to the side. This may take a little time to perfect but be patient. Just make sure you mark and praise them when they do it.

18. Once we are seeing a more relaxed posture we can add the cue 'Relax' or 'Chill', whichever you feel most comfortable with, but be consistent.

19. At this stage remember to use the cue just before you see your dog naturally performing the behaviour and pair being on the mat with a relaxing touch (such as an ear slide) or whatever you know relaxes them.

20. Once they are responding consistently (going to the mat and relaxing) you can fade out the training but rewards should still be given randomly and relaxing things should continue to be associated with it.

'Relax on a Mat' training, step 2. Introducing the dog to the mat.

'Relax on a Mat' training, step 7. Two paws on the mat.

'Relax on a Mat' training, step 10. All four paws on the mat.

'Relax on a Mat' training, step 16. Getting 'Down' on the mat.

The Emergency U-Turn

The idea of this training is to get a dog out of a problem situation quickly. It's also useful if you know that a dog is reaching their threshold for reactivity and they are going to be too highly aroused to respond to a 'Watch Me' or any other training cue. We need to teach a dog the 'Emergency U-turn' before using it for real otherwise it can startle them and may become a predictor that something scary is going to happen.

The Training Steps

1. With your dog on a lead, walk forward and use the verbal cue 'This way' in a calm and friendly tone.

2. Bend your knees as you turn as this avoids dragging them along. This is especially important for smaller breeds of dog.
3. Having a treat/toy in your hand can act as a lure to help back up the request.
4. Turn this into a fun game and remember to reward your dog immediately when they follow you.
5. The objective is to turn 180 degrees and move in the opposite direction.
6. As before, practise in places where you are free from distractions and build up slowly. The aim is for your dog to turn when you give the cue rather than being pulled forcibly away by you.
7. Gradually build up the training so that your dog moves a few more strides back with you before being given the reward.
8. Randomly ask for this on walks even when there is nothing going on. This helps it become a normal part of their exercise routine and won't startle them when you have to use it for real.
9. If you do have to use it in a real-life scenario try and use it proactively instead of reactively. In other words be observant of the dog's body language and the physical environment so you can pre-empt a problem. Getting out of the way before a dog goes over threshold is best.

(Guide adapted from *Feisty Fido: Help for the Leash-Reactive Dog* by Patricia B. McConnell and Karen B. London.)

'Emergency U-turn' training, step 1. It starts with walking forwards.

'Emergency U-turn' training, step 2. Initiate the turn, with bent knees.

'Emergency U-turn' training, step 5(a). Make the turn.

'Emergency U-turn' training, step 5(b). Travel back the way you came.

The 'Watch Me' Cue

Teaching a dog the 'Watch Me' means that we can get them to make eye contact on cue. This helps to gain their attention thereby providing a window of opportunity to ask them to do something else. This training also develops a dog's focus and control, which can be a useful way of conditioning frustration tolerance. As well as the practical applications for helping fearful and reactive dogs this training can be a useful exercise to include in a puppy's general training plan.

Other Benefits

- Teaching an alternative behaviour that isn't compatible with reactivity (such as jumping or lunging) means that we can set up new appropriate patterns of behaviour.
- As with 'What's That?' training, if we use it whenever the scary thing appears we can condition a dog to automatically look back at us in anticipation of good things happening, linking it to counter-conditioning training.

The Training Steps

1. Let your dog know you have a treat in your clenched fist and hold it out to the side at arm's length.
2. When your dog looks away from your hand and makes eye contact, to see why you haven't given them the food, immediately say 'Yes', and let them have the treat.
3. Extra help in the early stages of training is sometimes necessary. If your dog is having difficulties you may need to hold a treat closer to your face to get them started.
4. Repeat this exercise until they are consistently looking at you.
5. Now, as they look, add the cue 'Watch me' and reward as before.
6. Once a dog is consistently turning to look and understands the cue, it is possible to begin increasing the time they hold your gaze. Start with one second duration and increase second by second. Don't expect them to achieve more than three seconds in the early stages of training. If they lose interest,

slow things down. Any more than five seconds is too much.

7. Gradually generalize the behaviour in other locations where there are just a few more distractions but be prepared to go back a few steps in the training as it makes it harder for them to concentrate.

8. Expecting a very fearful, anxious or reactive dog to respond in an uncontrolled area is going to be too much to ask. Consider hiring a dog-walking field so you can practise in a controlled environment or seek the help of a professional trainer who has access to a safe and secure space to work. Later, as a dog progresses, they may be able to arrange 'stooges' (dogs or people).

9. Remember to make it easy for your dog to be successful. Do not be tempted to progress too quickly by taking them to a busy park or a town centre where there are lots of distractions.

'Watch Me' training, steps 4–6. Lots of genuine reward for eye contact.

10. Try to anticipate the moment the dog is about to turn its head toward the distraction and pulling very slightly on the lead, using your cue word 'Watch me'. Reward abundantly for the correct response.

11. If you know a situation is more than you can both handle, use the 'Emergency U-turn' training.

(Guide adapted from *Feisty Fido: Help for the Leash-Reactive Dog* by Patricia B. McConnell and Karen B. London.)

The 'What's That?' Cue

The idea of this training is to give a dog a cue to look at the object of their fear when they are under threshold and for you to mark and reward them when they do. This way they begin to link the presence of the scary thing with something good happening. It isn't suitable for dogs that are extremely reactive or dogs that use offensive aggression but it can help dogs that tend to avoid looking at something scary, which can make counter-conditioning more difficult.

Other Benefits

'Watch Me' training, step 1. The dog will look at the treat.

'Watch Me' training, step 3. You can hold the treat closer to your face to help them look at you, if needed.

- It conditions a dog to look back at us in anticipation of good things happening when they see the scary thing in the environment, giving us some control and linking in with counter-conditioning.
- It gives a dog a greater sense of control over their environment.

- The way a dog responds helps us assess how they feel and this opens up the lines of communication.

The Training Steps

1. Find somewhere safe and free from distractions. The dog must be relaxed and below threshold.
2. It's better for this training to begin working with 'stooges'. Control the distance between the dog and the 'stooge'.
3. To encourage a dog to look at the 'scary thing' create some movement. For example ask a 'stooge' to walk or move around (with a dog if that is the object of their fear) or even make a noise (not too loud) so they take notice.
4. Timing is crucial. As they look in the direction, mark with 'Yes' or 'Good' (or a clicker).
5. As they turn to look at you, reward with a highly valued reward. What we want is to teach them that looking at the scary thing, and then back at you, is what gets them the reward.
6. Repeat this process, making sure they stay under threshold.
7. Don't be in a rush to move the target closer. The idea at this stage is just to reward the dog every time they look at the frightening stimulus.
8. Once they are doing this consistently, add the cue, 'What's that?' in a happy, relaxed tone of voice.
9. If a dog stares, becomes aroused, stops taking treats or won't play, you will need to take a step back in

'What's That?' training, step 5. Looking back at you.

the training and increase the distance from the target. This two-way conversation builds trust and enhances their sense of security.

10. Once a dog is trained, they begin automatically to turn to look at us when they see the scary thing, in anticipation of a reward. This is what we want.
11. This training can be used alongside 'Watch Me'. Having the option of both cues can be helpful.

(Guide adapted from *Feisty Fido: Help for the Leash-Reactive Dog* by Patricia B. McConnell and Karen B. London.)

The 'Come Away' Cue

The principle behind this training is to teach a dog to come away from things and return to you. In this way they look to you to make decisions about what to do next. Before embarking on this training it is important to be familiar with using a long-line lead.

The Benefits

- A useful way of getting a dog to return to us when we encounter a situation that we know may cause them distress.
- Helps when working with critical distances during programmes of desensitization and counter-conditioning (DS CC).
- Useful for getting a dog to come away from something that may be potentially dangerous.

'What's That?' training, step 4. Looking at the object of fear.

The Training Steps

1. Allow the dog to walk around and explore whilst attached to a long lead of around 5m (16ft) in length.
2. Regularly stop and 'lock' the leash without causing any excessive pulling or jolting the dog.
3. Take a few paces backwards, saying 'Come away' in a calm but friendly tone.
4. When your dog turns to come, praise them.
5. Once they return to you, give a number of food rewards.
6. Shape the training so that they can wait at your side for a few seconds longer.
7. Give them a release signal such as 'Off you go'.
8. This training can be modified to ask the dog for a 'Touch' or a 'Watch me' cue once they are by your side.

'Come Away' training, step 3. Call them away.

9. When the dog is able to perform the behaviour consistently, in different locations and with a few more distractions, it can be used as part of a DS CC programme of training.

(Guide adapted from 'The Come Away Command' in *Behaviour Problems in Small Animals: Practical Advice for the Veterinary Team* by Jon Bowen and Sarah Heath.)

Hand Target Training (Touch)

Hand target training involves a dog targeting (touching) the palm of your hand with their nose. This training can be modified to use other objects such as a target stick or a cone on the ground but using a hand is ideal because it means we don't need to carry anything around with us, which makes life easier if we have a dog that needs careful handling.

The Benefits

- Having a simple cue like 'Touch' can be a useful strategy for distracting a dog.
- Asking a dog to focus on touching a hand is incompatible with inappropriate behaviours such as staring, hypervigilance, lunging and barking.
- It helps to keep them focused and engages the brain which can prevent them from going over threshold and reacting inappropriately.
- Following and targeting a hand means we can move a dog to a further distance from the object of their fear.

'Come Away' training, step 1. A long-line lead is useful for training this cue.

'Come Away' training, step 2. Gently stop the dog.

- It can be used in conjunction with an 'Emergency U-turn' and 'Come Away' training to help back up the cues and in pattern games to add another dimension to the training.

The Training Steps

1. Hold out your hand so the dog can see it (without thrusting it in their face) and once they move towards it to investigate or sniff it, mark the behaviour by saying 'Yes' or 'Good' and follow this up with a reward.
2. I prefer to drop the treat on the floor so that they have to physically move back towards the hand in the next bout of training.
3. If the dog has real difficulty, you can smear something tasty on the hand to get them started. That isn't cheating, it's just helping them to orientate to your hand so they understand what you want but you shouldn't need to do this for long.
4. Repeat this sequence many times: Dog touches with their nose. Mark with your verbal cue and treat.
5. Move your hand around and practise a little further away from the dog so they have to move a bit further towards the target.
6. Once the dog is consistently moving forward and touching the palm of the hand with their nose – add a cue (such as 'Touch').
7. We should have the following sequence: hand presented, the dog moves forward and just as they are touching we say 'Touch' and the reward is given.
8. Keep up with this training, using the cue regularly.

9. Eventually it can be used in more distracting circumstances and in real-life situations.

Hand target training, step 2. Dropping the treat.

Hand target training, step 5. Moving the target.

Hand target training, steps 6–7. Adding the cue of 'Touch' (or whatever you choose).

Hand target training, step 1. Reward investigation initially.

The 'Settle' Cue

This training technique will, if practised regularly, help to change the dog's mood so that a settled and calm state can be put on cue.

Benefits

- It can be used to help a dog settle down following a frightening incident or prevent an escalation of arousal and fear.
- It can be used at the end of a play session so that the dog knows when play time is finished. This prevents them from becoming frustrated.

The Training Steps

1. Play a game with the dog that you know will get them excited.
2. A signal such as 'Let's play' can be used.
3. After about a minute of play but before they get over excited, become very calm and stop the game, using the verbal cue, 'Settle' or whatever you choose, but be consistent.
4. Whilst the dog is gradually coming down from their high arousal, give them food treats as a reward.
5. Don't give the treats if they are still aroused and don't start to play again until the dog is calm.
6. Give the signal as before and start the process again.
7. For several minutes keep alternating between playing and being calm, still using the treats as a reward for calmness.
8. Finish the game by encouraging the dog to be calm for a number of rewards and then offer them something to chew and lick to occupy them.
9. This routine teaches the dog to end the game, anticipating something good but calming rather than expecting another bout of play.
10. Eventually, the training can be phased out but only once they are recognizing and responding to the cue.

Regular practice will ensure that the dog quickly responds to the signal and it can then be used in other situations when the dog becomes excited or agitated.

(Guide adapted from 'The Come Away Command' in *Behaviour Problems in Small Animals: Practical Advice for the Veterinary Team* by Jon Bowen and Sarah Heath.)

House-Line Training

The house-line is a useful way of controlling a dog without using force or direct physical contact, which can be perceived as a threat.

Times when you may need to use a house-line include:

- Working with nervous or newly adopted dogs.
- To control a dog or remove them from danger (for example during a phobic episode).
- As a safety measure (for example in combination with 'Meeting Visitors in the Home').
- To help back up a cue.

The house-line is fixed to the dog's collar and left to trail along behind them but only when they are being supervised. A house-line should never be used when the dog is alone.

The Training Steps

1. Gently take the end of the house-line, avoiding eye contact.
2. Walk away from the dog but avoid pulling or yanking it.
3. Using a calm tone, call the dog using a cue that you want them to respond to. For example: 'Rosie, here' for a recall.
4. When the dog responds to the cue, turn around to face them and follow up with a reward.
5. If the dog does not respond, repeat the request, still using a calm tone, and act in a relaxed manner.
6. If the dog fails to respond, the line is now tensed and a couple of gentle tugs are used to dislodge the dog, giving the cue so that the dog can associate it with the action.
7. Turn and reward the dog as soon as they perform the desired response.

Pulling at the dog whilst staring at them can be very challenging and some dogs will take this as a direct threat and may become fear aggressive. Try to remain calm throughout this training and if the dog does not respond, do not allow your voice to get louder or threatening. To avoid injury or inducing a fear response, be gentle but do continue to exert some pressure on the line until they stop resisting. The line should never be associated with pain or appear threatening.

(Guide adapted from 'Using a Houseline' in *Behaviour Problems in Small Animals: Practical Advice for the Veterinary Team by* Jon Bowen and Sarah Heath.)

Meeting Visitors In The Home

This guide is designed to help dogs that get anxious or fearful when visitors come to the home. However, this training isn't suitable for extremely fearful or fear-aggressive dogs. In those circumstances management is best; protecting them and others should be a priority. Cameras with movement sensors at the front door can pre-warn that visitors are coming so that dogs can be led away somewhere safe, quiet and comfortable. Before embarking on the training you must be familiar with using a house-line and when working with people, as an added safety measure, it is advisable to have the dog muzzled. Therefore they must be fully muzzle trained and you must use 'stooge visitors' who are well versed in the training.

The Training Steps

1. Seeing a person entering their home can be a source of anxiety, so do not allow the dog to meet visitors at the door or other boundaries to the property.

2. Before the 'visitors' arrive, have the dog in another room away from the main entrance where they are unable to see them arriving.

3. Give them an interactive feeder or set something up that will occupy them.

4. If the dog is barking or vocalizing when visitors arrive at the door, do not shout as this can heighten their distress.

5. Once the dog is calm and the 'visitors' are in the home, sat down and settled, attach the house-line (and muzzle if necessary) and allow the dog to see them.

6. Tell the visitors to ignore the dog and to only show them mild interest to start with.

7. Keep eye contact to a minimum.

8. Keep the dog close to you so that you can control it easily. You could place a foot over the line as an added precaution.

9. Arm the 'visitors' with very tasty treats but they must not lure the dog.

10. Let the dog approach the 'visitor' rather than the 'visitor' approach them.

11. As long as the dog is calm and not showing any signs of fear, they can gently throw a treat to the ground, a little distance away.

12. Keep interactions positive and calm – if the dog approaches the 'visitor' in a friendly manner or

Meeting visitors in the home training, step 8. Keep gentle control of the dog with a foot over their house line.

comes for another treat then the 'visitor' can interact a little more.

13. Take it slowly, no sudden movements and keep hands and fingers out of the way. Presenting the back of the hand with the fist clenched for them to sniff is less threatening.

14. Make sure the 'visitor' doesn't touch them around the head or bring their hand down from above the dog as this can be perceived as threatening.

15. Do not allow a dog to jump up onto the sofa or be at face height with the 'visitor' as this is potentially dangerous.

16. Some dogs react when the 'visitor' leaves. Sudden movements and standing up can be a trigger for fear so it is advisable to use the house-line to control them or lead the dog away before the 'visitor' gets up to leave or use the bathroom.

(Guide adapted from *Behaviour Problems in Small Animals: Practical Advice for the Veterinary Team by* Jon Bowen and Sarah Heath.)

Pattern Games

The concept of pattern games was introduced by Leslie McDevitt, an American-based dog trainer. There are numerous games to choose from, each providing a dog with a predictable and secure structure to follow. Here are a couple adapted from Leslie's book, which I highly recommend you take a look at.

Benefits

- To get a dog away from something scary.
- To help a dog focus on something else whilst getting past something scary.
- When working on programmes of DS and CC.
- Gives a dog some control over whether they wish to move forward.

The Training Steps

1. Get the dog's interest by using their favourite treats. Whilst they are in front of you, say out loud: 'One', 'Two', 'Three', and on three, drop a tasty treat on the floor for the dog to retrieve.
2. Do this for a few repetitions.

3. Next add movement – take three steps, still counting to three out loud.
4. On three, place the treat on the ground and stop.
5. Before starting the pattern again, wait for the dog to offer you their eye contact.
6. Before long they will start looking up at you as they begin to anticipate the cycle being repeated.
7. The voluntary offering of eye contact dictates when you move forward and in this way the dog can communicate their consent, giving them control over the situation.
8. The sequence is: one, two – drop the treat on three. Stop. When the dog looks up at you, you can move forward – repeat the sequence.
9. Try and create a rhythm and flow to the game. Keep their interest by giving them lots of encouragement.
10. Now begin to practise this in slightly more distracting environments – when they look up, move forward. If not, give them a little more time to process what's going on.
11. Gradually, you can work with more distractions.
12. Eventually these games can be used during desensitization and counter-conditioning training sessions.
13. If you see danger ahead, pre-empt the situation so that you do not lead them into difficulties. Use any of the other management tools such as the 'Emergency U-turn' or 'Come Away'.

Variations

- If a dog has already been taught, incorporating a hand 'Touch' can add another dimension to the

Pattern games – count 'one'.

Pattern games – count 'two'.

Pattern games – count 'three' and drop treat.

Targeting adds another dimension to pattern games.

training. The sequence would be repeated as above, but this time add a 'Touch' cue after the count of three, followed by the reward.

- Using props such as sports cones laid on the ground or held for a dog to target can also provide another focus.

Once mastered, this training can be used whenever you anticipate a difficult situation and can help to distract and capture their interest as well as moving them away from difficulties.

(Guide adapted from the '1, 2, 3 Pattern Game' in *Control Unleashed* by Leslie McDevitt.)

Socialization Checklist

Examples of who and what things a puppy should be introduced to during their socialization period.

Meeting People

- ✓ People of all genders, ethnicities and ages, including babies, toddlers, children and the elderly
- ✓ People wearing glasses and sunglasses
- ✓ People with different hairstyles and facial hair
- ✓ People wearing hats, hoods, turbans and other headgear
- ✓ People wearing high-visibility clothing
- ✓ People in Halloween masks and other fancy dress
- ✓ People with walking frames and walking sticks and in, or pushing, a wheelchair or pram
- ✓ People riding bicycles or on a skateboard
- ✓ People walking or running past
- ✓ People in uniforms or other work clothing (including veterinary uniforms)
- ✓ People carrying bags, backpacks and wheeling shopping trolleys
- ✓ Veterinary personnel
- ✓ People in shops (including shopkeepers behind counters)

Introducing Animals

- ✓ Other friendly and vaccinated dogs of various size, shape, age and colour (on and off-lead)
- ✓ Horses in fields and being ridden
- ✓ Sheep, cattle and other livestock

- ✓ Cats
- ✓ Small mammals including rabbits, guinea pigs and so on

Noises

- ✓ Alarm clocks, smoke and burglar alarms
- ✓ Animal noises, such as other dogs, horses, donkeys, cats
- ✓ Babies crying and vocalizing
- ✓ Children playing
- ✓ Door bells
- ✓ Traffic on dry and wet surfaces
- ✓ Small kitchen appliances, for example blenders, electric whisks
- ✓ Cooking noises
- ✓ Large kitchen appliances, for example washing machine, tumble dryers
- ✓ Hairdryers
- ✓ Roadworks, for example pneumatic drills
- ✓ Ambulance and other emergency vehicle sirens
- ✓ Music of all genres
- ✓ Lawn mowers and other garden appliances
- ✓ Thunder
- ✓ Fireworks
- ✓ Gunshot and bird-scarers
- ✓ Vacuum cleaners

Surfaces

- ✓ Bark chippings
- ✓ Different heights
- ✓ Grass (living and artificial)
- ✓ Carpet
- ✓ Tiles (slippery and non-slip)
- ✓ Laminate/wooden
- ✓ Uneven and wobbly
- ✓ Wet and muddy

Handling and Restraint

- ✓ Being touched on all body parts (including feet and nails)
- ✓ Being handled and restrained for examination (to include seeing and feeling a stethoscope on their body and having eyes and ears examined)
- ✓ The sensation of wearing a collar, harness and lead

✓ Wearing a coat or medical vest
✓ Being groomed and bathed
✓ Being touched by all categories of people

Different Places, Situations and Environments

✓ Children's play park
✓ Doggy play park
✓ Towns, cities and the countryside
✓ The beach
✓ Shops and shopping malls, public houses and restaurants
✓ Veterinary clinic
✓ Grooming parlour
✓ Boarding kennels
✓ Dens, crates and so on
✓ Different weather conditions, for example wind, rain
✓ Travelling, for example bus, car, coach, train
✓ Seeing the full range of vehicles, for example lorries, vans, emergency vehicles with flashing lights, tractors, dustbin trailers, caravans
✓ Playing with different toys including ones that squeak

✓ Training classes and puppy socialization parties (well-run ones!)
✓ Having visitors and gatherings of people

Tips

- Everything should be introduced gradually and in a controlled manner.
- Create some distance between each stimulus and mute noises to begin with to ensure that experiences are not overwhelming.
- A puppy must be relaxed, doing something pleasing or having fun at the same time they are being exposed to a situation.
- Observe them constantly and immediately stop what you are doing if they show any signs of stress. Go back to a stage they are comfortable with and progress more slowly.
- Revisit socialization experiences throughout and beyond the socialization period, right up until the dog reaches adulthood. Otherwise the positive effects can wane.
- Although it is important to include a raft of experiences, it's the quality of the experience that really matters.

CHAPTER 11

Case Studies

This selection of case studies provides a basic summary of the types of fear-related problems that a behaviourist may have to deal with and the sample behaviour modification plans (BMP) are designed to give the reader a flavour of what is significant to a case and what can be done. However, the rest of the book and the training guides (Chapter 10) provide a more comprehensive account of the particulars required to implement the plans and various other treatment options are available for consideration, particularly with regard to complementary and integrated adjuncts.

Inevitably desensitization and counter-conditioning (DS CC) will be a fundamental part of all the BMPs and each case will be approached in a similar manner. To avoid repetition, for each case, the following assumptions should be made:

- The cases have been referred by a veterinary surgeon. All the dogs have undergone a clinical examination to rule out any medical problems and have been given a suitable non-prescription nutraceutical for their calming properties.
- All owners have been taught how to recognize canine communication signals.
- Unless otherwise noted all the dogs are being fed a suitable diet.
- A programme of mental and physical enrichment has been integrated into each plan.
- The 'suitable training techniques' have been demonstrated and have begun and owners are being supported in order to develop their training skills.

Opposite: Zara, courtesy of Amanda Dobbs.

- Owners are conversant with the principles of training as outlined in the 'Tips for Training' guide and the 'Life Reward' training, referred to in Chapter 8, has been implemented in all their dogs' daily routines.
- Owners know they must not proceed to the next stage until they have undertaken all the recommended training in the previous stage.

I have only shown up to stage three in the BMP although, in reality, there may be many more stages.

Common Approaches to Behaviour Modification

- Rule out medical problems
- Allow the dog to have some respite from stressors whilst owners are preparing equipment and practising training skills
- Identify triggers
- Arrange the environment/s
- Consider the impact of human behaviour
- Provide mental and physical enrichment
- Teach a dog new behaviours that are incompatible with inappropriate ones
- Implement DS and CC techniques
- Review and modify the diet
- Consider adjuncts based on the dog's requirements
- Monitor and log progress

I have also given an overview of how the plan might progress in the future. For details of the recommended training techniques, please refer to the training guides in Chapter 10.

Case Study 1: Holly, an Eleven-Month-Old Female Labrador

Background
Holly had developed a degree of anxiety when she was taken outside the house for walks, most notably hyper-vigilance and scanning behaviours. According to the owners, her behaviour had worsened over the previous four months or so and they were beginning to notice that she was less relaxed in the house.

Holly's most marked reaction is when she sees horses loose in the field. This is difficult to avoid as the owners live in a countryside setting, popular with horse riders.

Case Study 1: Holly – Fear of horses.

Her behaviour changes once she is within about 9m (30ft) from them. Initially she becomes alert, then seems reluctant to move in their direction and the closer she gets, the more agitated she becomes. The owners had tried to get her used to them by taking her for daily walks in areas where they knew horses would be grazing but things hadn't improved. Now Holly seems reluctant to go for walks.

The owners reported that Holly had been well socialized and they had been diligent in this since getting her as a nine-week-old puppy. Holly had always been very relaxed when introduced to new situations and would happily deal well with most things, so they were perplexed at the change in her behaviour. She had also seen horses before and had shown no fear of them up until about six months ago, just prior to coming into season, when she had been chased across a field by one. The owners said it was quite frightening and they had been screaming at her to come back as they were worried she was going to be kicked. Holly is more fearful of horses when she sees them moving but what the owners find strange is that she doesn't seem as bothered by them when she sees them through the window being ridden past the house. Holly can also cope with them outside, provided they are not being ridden directly towards her. Holly loves her food and likes playing with her ball, especially one that squeaks.

Significant Information

- Being chased by the horse seems to have been the major trigger for Holly's behaviour change.
- Holly had just been coming in to season when the incident occurred. It is therefore likely that the whole experience will have felt even more traumatic for her.
- Holly is still is in the sensitive developmental period of adolescence.
- The owners are taking Holly to see the horses on a daily basis, which will be sensitizing and possibly flooding her.
- Holly's behaviour is very context specific so work on DS and CC can be targeted.
- Holly is at 'threshold' at around 9m (30ft) from the target of her fear.
- The rewards that will aid Holly's training programme have been identified.

Diagnosis and Discussion

Although this was clearly a single-event learning experience, the sudden onset of other fear-related problems are suggestive of post-traumatic stress disorder (PTSD), as described in Chapter 2. Holly is still an adolescent and therefore it is of the utmost importance to address this situation quickly, but sensitively, before things worsen.

The BMP

The initial aim is to give Holly some time to emotionally 'decompress' and support her mental well-being. Stripping back and reintroducing Holly to situations as if she were a puppy should help to reset and help her through adolescence. We can then implement a programme of training, making sure she is having fun but, at the same time, is learning cues that have a practical element to them. The rest of the plan centres on gradual exposure towards the area where the incident took place and even more gradual exposure to horses, using DS and CC in a staged and controlled way. The distance from the horses where Holly is at 'threshold' is about 9m (30ft), so our start point should be at least 12m (40ft) away (or where she is relaxed and comfortable).

Suitable training techniques

- ✓ 'Come Away'
- ✓ 'Relax on a Mat'
- ✓ 'Watch Me'/'What's That?'
- ✓ 'Settle' cue
- ✓ 'Emergency U-turn'
- ✓ Pattern games
- ✓ Desensitization and counter-conditioning (DS CC) to horses

Stage one

- Avoid going to places where Holly has had any negative associations with horses.
- Take Holly out for walks to locations where she can relax and have fun with her squeaky toy. This should help redress negative associations with going out on walks.
- Capture and reward relaxed body postures and behaviours, including when the horses ride by the window.
- Use 'Relax on a Mat' in the home.

- Revisit socialization techniques, introducing Holly to new experiences very slowly and sensitively.
- Teach pattern games and consider an activity such as Mantrailing which may provide a safe and fun outlet. Use the 'Settle' cue after play.

Stage two

- Return to familiar walks but remain in areas where she cannot see the horses.
- Practise the 'Watch Me'/'What's That?', 'Emergency U-turn' and 'Come Away' randomly, remembering to turn them into a fun game using her squeaky toy or food as a reward.

Stage three

- Begin DS. Find a suitable venue where horses can be seen but not the venue where the frightening incident occurred to begin with.
- Use the long-line and, staying well within the critical distance, use the 'Come away' cue.
- Use 'Watch Me'/'What's That?' training.
- Play pattern games.
- After a period of training and play, spread out the comfort mat and induce relaxation using the 'Settle' cue and 'Relax on a Mat'. Work can then begin on CC.

Making Progress with the Plan

Continue this training plan and slowly and gradually reduce the distance between the horses and Holly. Provided Holly continues to make progress, DS and CC can begin around the field where the incident occurred. However, care must be taken as returning to the place where the traumatic experience occurred may cause her to have a flashback.

As Holly is better with stationary horses, sudden movement is likely to put the training back. Enlisting the help of a horse owner who would be prepared to restrain a horse behind a fenced enclosure so it isn't able to move freely may prove helpful.

Walking through a field of loose horses is probably always going to be a step too far and is potentially dangerous. Avoiding this using proper restraint and management is a sensible precaution.

Case Study 2: Boris, A Six-Year-Old Male (Neutered) Golden Retriever

Background

Boris lives with his owner, a single lady who has had him from a puppy. Boris never had a problem with being left alone until his owner spent a year working from home during the COVID-19 pandemic. His owner reported that Boris spent most of his time in close contact with her during the time she was at home and now shadows her almost constantly. However, he does sleep overnight in his travel crate on the landing and not in the owner's bedroom.

Since the behaviour began, two months ago, video cameras have been set up when Boris is left alone. He remains agitated for the first half hour and then settles for short periods. Noises outside regularly wake him and

Case Study 2: Boris – Separation anxiety. (Photo courtesy of Evonne Randall)

he then begins to whine and pace for half-hour periods before settling again but he never seems to fully rest. There hasn't been any real destruction in the house but when he began to chew a leg of the coffee table he was chastised and restricted to the kitchen.

Boris is not showing any other anxious behaviours but does begin to exhibit signs of stress and maintains a close proximity to the owner as she is preparing to go out to work. It can take his owner quite a while to leave as she has to coax him into the kitchen and then tucks him up in his bed. Boris is always extremely excited when his owner comes home but his owner ignores him for at least the first fifteen minutes as she read somewhere that this would help.

Recently, when the owner had to visit her mother over-night, Boris stayed with a friend without any problems. Boris is a sociable dog who enjoys his food. Cheese is his favourite treat.

Significant Information

- Boris almost constantly shadows his owner.
- The initial trigger for Boris was the change to his owner's working routine.
- Getting ready for work seems to be a predictive cue to being left and causes Boris some anxiety.
- Noises outside are current triggers.
- Boris has been restricted to the kitchen, which is causing him some distress.
- Chewing behaviour on the coffee table may have been a coping mechanism to alleviate stress.
- Boris is not hyper-attached to his owner and can be left comfortably with other people.
- Boris is not resting so is likely to be fatigued.
- Cheese can be used as a reward during training sessions.
- The owner has sought help early on in Boris's problematic behaviour, which makes for a better prognosis.

Diagnosis and Discussion

Boris appears to be demonstrating moderate levels of separation anxiety (SA). At this stage, helping him become less dependent on the owner and building up his confidence when he is alone is a significant part of the plan. Desensitization techniques will underpin the treatment and for that it's crucial that Boris is in a relaxing environment. It is also important to monitor his behaviour through a camera in real time to ensure that he remains below threshold and so his owner can return before he becomes anxious.

In severe cases, a dog should not be left alone beyond their ability to cope. This is because if the dog is making good progress with a training programme, but in between sessions they become extremely distressed, their improvement will suffer. Regular monitoring of Boris's progress is important. If his symptoms worsen, getting some help from dog walkers, doggy day care providers or calling on friends and family to dog sit may become a necessary part of the plan. Where this is not possible, or for dogs that are unable to learn new behaviours because of their level of distress, veterinary prescribed medication may be required.

The BMP

Suitable training techniques

- ✓ 'Settle cue'
- ✓ 'Relax on a Mat'
- ✓ Desensitization and counter-conditioning to the baby gate, the treat dispensing device (if one is going to be used as part of the plan) and, ultimately, to being left alone.

Arranging antecedents and managing the triggers forms a large part of this plan and Boris must be comfortable and relaxed where he is going to be left. Dog appeasing pheromone therapy and natural calming dietary supplements may help a little, as might playing calming background music or audiobook recordings. However, being confined to the kitchen is clearly a source of anxiety for Boris so this needs addressing.

It's common for a dog to become distressed ahead of a departure, so changing routines and muddling cues should prevent Boris from getting more anxious as he sees his owner prepare to leave. This doesn't mean slipping out unnoticed because, for some dogs, finding themselves suddenly alone can be a cause for alarm. It's more about diverting his attention towards something engaging. Therefore, another part of the plan is encouraging independent self-reinforcing activities.

These can then be used as a distraction whilst the owner gets ready to leave. Being organized, and preparing things the night before to make the process shorter, is another part of the management. Mental and physical exercise helps to tire a dog, so taking Boris out for some exercise before leaving him alone would be another recommendation.

Farewells should be fairly brief and adopting a more jolly and matter-of-fact approach is better than prolonged goodbyes. Scattering food and setting up seek and find exercises might turn the event into something much more positive. However these activities should be implemented regularly, not just when leaving him alone, as dogs can soon begin to predict these rituals as a prelude to being left alone.

Although frenzied greetings should be discouraged, using extinction is unlikely to help. Teaching a 'Settle' and/or using the baby gate to stop him jumping up, as well as teaching him a 'Sit' and 'Wait' cue, would help cultivate a long-term solution. In the interim, timing greetings to when all his four paws are on the ground and greeting him warmly, but calmly, should help reinforce a more appropriate response.

Stage one

- Stop chastising (P+) Boris as this will increase his anxiety.
- Introduce and teach mentally enriching independent activities.
- Redirect chewing behaviours towards interactive feeders (with cheese and other tasty rewards) and toys.
- Address the physical environments:

  - ✓ Install and introduce baby gates but don't shut them to begin with.
  - ✓ Manage noises from outside, for example use heavy blackout curtains, mask sounds with background music or audio-books.
  - ✓ Stop confining Boris to the kitchen (move the coffee table).
  - ✓ Surround Boris with things he is allowed to chew.
  - ✓ Use his night-time crate to create a safe haven/den (moving it downstairs during the day if necessary).

✓ A piece of the owner's clothing, tucked in his bedding, may provide a familiar scent and provide some comfort.

- Capture and reward Boris when he is chewing his toys, engaging in independent activities, and relaxing inside his travel crate.
- Implement 'Relax on a Mat' training and then use the same comfort mat/blanket inside his crate to induce calmness.

Stage two

- Use the 'Settle' cue to help prevent frenzied greetings.
- Integrate 'seek and find' games into his daily routine.
- Whilst Boris is engaged in independent self-reinforcing activities, very briefly (two to three seconds) close the baby gate and make some in-sight departures.
- Gradually increase the duration and distance from the gate but still remain in-sight.

Stage three

- Continue work on the training in stage one and two.
- Practice brief (two to three second) out of sight departures. This involves shutting the baby gate and moving somewhere where Boris is unable to see the owner.
- Continue work on DS and CC techniques, very gradually extending the time Boris is left alone.
- Use a variable reinforcement schedule to fluctuate between very brief departures and slightly longer ones. This means Boris will be less able to predict the length of time he is going to be left alone.
- As the duration increases, real-time video recordings will be required to assess Boris remotely. The owner must return before any signs of anxiety are noted.
- Consider using remote-control treat dispensing devices that can be set to eject a reward at timed intervals. These can assist in raising the duration criteria (whilst the dog waits for the reward) as well as distract them. The noise they emit can be startling so carrying out some DS may be required beforehand.

Making Progress with the Plan

Provided Boris is making progress, work can begin on staged departures from the house. Owners must always be prepared to go back in the plan where necessary.

If Boris's behaviour worsened or there was no significant improvement in between his training sessions it would be worth discussing other adjuncts. Veterinary medication may help but because the most effective treatments take around six weeks to reach their therapeutic effect, doggy day care would be a recommendation and required for at least that period and, depending on his response, possibly longer.

Case Study 3: Zak, an Approximately Three-Year-Old Male (Neutered) Romanian Rescue Dog

Background

Zak lived life as a street dog in Romania until he was rescued and brought to the UK seven months previously. Zak spent the first four months in a shelter, which had been a source of stress for him but he was then moved to foster carers (a husband-and-wife team) just after being surgically castrated. He has been in their care for three months and is coping fairly well. He likes his crate and is happy to go there with an interactive feeder and this is where he relaxes and sleeps.

Case Study 3: Zak the street dog – Generalized anxiety. (Photo courtesy of Tommy Taylor)

Zak's issue is fearfulness of unfamiliar men and this is problematic when he encounters them on walks. His reactions can be described as avoidant and when he sees them getting closer, he tries to dash to the opposite side of the road or behind the legs of the carer for protection. Recently he snapped at a male jogger who appeared suddenly from a side street but fortunately he didn't make contact with their skin. The only place he is relaxed is at the local beach and, as it is off-season, it is quiet so he can run on his fully extended flexi-lead, which he loves. He doesn't know how to play with toys but seems very comfortable meeting other dogs that approach him.

With a sensitive approach he quickly became at ease around the male foster carer, although he prefers to approach him on his own terms. Zak isn't fond of eye contact or too much physical contact. He is mildly stressed when female visitors come to the house but, as a safety measure, when male visitors come, he is contained in a crate. The carers ask male visitors to drop his favourite treats (dried liver) through the bars to try and desensitize him but he hides under the bedding and only eats when they have gone.

Significant Information

Zak has undergone a number of traumatic events in a short space of time.

- Zak has been castrated which may affect his level of confidence.
- His main target of fear is unfamiliar men.
- Zak is being confined in his crate (in full sight of male visitors) which is clearly fear-inducing and may create negative associations with it.
- Zak quickly became comfortable around the male foster carer.
- Zak is not comfortable with eye or physical contact and prefers to approach on his terms.
- He has already shown some fear-aggression.
- He is being exercised on a flexi-lead.
- He loves the beach and enjoys running.
- He likes dried liver.

Diagnosis and Discussion

This is a fear-related problem that could very easily develop into a more challenging case of fear-aggression. Zak's lack of habituation and experience of being handled and kept as a pet dog is most probably at the root of the problem. It is also possible that he had a negative experience with a man in his past. In view of the traumatic experiences he has already endured, PTSD should also be on the radar.

Zak will have inevitably missed being habituated and socialized to certain stimuli that would be familiar to a 'normal' domestic dog. Therefore, the BMP should take this into account. In their familiar environment, street dogs tend to cope with stress and conflict well. This is largely because, in that context, they have the freedom to make choices. Once restrained they lose their main coping strategies: avoidance and escape. Having no sense of control means they can become fearful and sometimes frustrated.

As Zak is not comfortable with eye contact, using 'Watch Me' might be intimidating in the early stages of his training. However, pattern games might encourage him to begin to make some eye contact on his own terms and will introduce him to play.

Locations where there are lots of people, in confined spaces and with narrow pavements and blind corners, are best avoided. To safeguard Zak and the public, I would advise that he is always muzzled when he is in public places and resources such as those available through The Yellow Dog Project would be useful.

The BMP

Suitable training techniques

- ✓ 'Muzzle' training
- ✓ 'Come Away'
- ✓ 'Emergency U-turn'
- ✓ Pattern games
- ✓ Desensitization and counter-conditioning to a harness and unfamiliar men
- ✓ Behaviour Adjustment Training (BAT)

Central to Zak's BMP is DS and CC but when the target of fear includes people, this can be dangerous. Therefore focusing on health and safety is an early step, as is working on better control methods. Establishing the critical distance where Zak remains below threshold is going to be important for working on DS and CC.

The plan also needs to restore his sense of freedom and to give him back the chance to say 'No' and for this to be recognized by the carer. If not, he may adopt aggressive behaviours in order to cope with the problem and this may become self-reinforcing. BAT could easily be integrated into a plan of this kind.

Zak appears to be relaxed around other dogs so finding friendly dogs for him to mix with, in a controlled environment, may provide an outlet for play and enhance his well-being.

Stage one

- Follow a programme of socialization and introduce Zak to new experiences very slowly and sensitively.
- Avoid walking him in busy places where he is likely to come into contact with strangers. If a safe and controlled environment cannot be arranged, groundwork, based on the TTouch or ACE free style principles, can be set up in the home and garden.
- Continue DS and CC to the harness and 'Muzzle training' before taking him to public places.
- Create positive associations with the crate to help offset any negative associations he may have been developing with it. (Refer to 'Crate Training' in Chapter 10.)
- Regularly use the long-line and 'Come Away' training in safe and quiet places.
- In advance of visitors arriving to the house put Zak in a familiar and quiet room, well away from them, with an interactive feeder and access to his crate.
- Swap the flexi-lead for a double-clip lead.
- Begin some pattern games.
- Capture and reinforce Zak's behaviour whenever he sees anyone in the distance and remains calm.

Stage two

- Randomly and regularly use the 'Emergency U-turn' and 'Come Away' cues.
- If safe to do so, take Zak to the beach at quiet times, when the tide is fully out. Having Zak muzzled and safely controlled on a long-line, with a wide expanse of sand, means handlers (and Zak) can safely see what is going on.

- In combination with the 'Emergency U-turn' and 'Come Away' training, BAT principles can be utilized.

Stage three

- When Zak is responding consistently to the 'Come Away', 'Emergency U-turns' and 'BAT' training, work can begin on DS and CC to unfamiliar males in controlled spaces.
- Set up scenarios with male 'stooges' (who are familiar with the training) and communicate via a mobile phone to control the pace.
- Mark and reward Zak for low-intensity, calm behaviours.

Making Progress with the Plan

If this plan is too restrictive in terms of having to arrange venues and involving 'stooges' it might fail. Foster carers may find it too imposing on their time and a new owner might be put off taking him on. The last thing we want is for Zak to be sent back to a rescue environment. Therefore, working in quiet public places (like the beach in off-season, quiet periods) is another possibility *provided* all the safety measures have been fulfilled and he is managed properly so that he remains below threshold.

The decision whether to let Zak meet unfamiliar males in the house should be discussed as his progress unfolds. (Refer to the 'Meeting Visitors in the Home' training guide in Chapter 10.)

For practical purposes, it is important to be able to touch a dog. Therefore DS and CC to human touch should be included in his training programme, but not until he has built trust with his human carer. Waiting for him to approach and applying a light, very brief, touch on his shoulder can be marked and rewarded. To avoid startling Zak a cue such as 'Contact' can be used so that he is aware that he is going to be touched beforehand.

Dogs like Zak can often be passed from home to home simply because new owners don't know how to manage their problems. Being given a clear and honest account of his needs when finding him his forever home is paramount. Zak would probably suit someone who enjoys an active lifestyle. In the right setting he might take to CaniCross. Living near a beach would be the 'cherry on the cake', but the main aim is finding someone who can be sympathetic to his needs.

Case Study 4: Ash, A Ten-Year-Old Male (Neutered) Staffordshire Bull Terrier

Background

Ash has sound sensitivity and generalized anxiety. Things developed after a family camping holiday the previous September. The owners recalled that a sausage on the barbeque spat at him and he yelped and ran away but at the time, they didn't think anything of it. Afterwards, they began to notice that he seemed anxious upon hearing the noise of the sizzling food and towards the end of the holiday he would try to get back inside the tent whenever the BBQ was lit.

At home things developed further. He was reluctant to go in the garden when the hosepipe was in use, and during firework season he was reactive to the noise of fireworks, which had only bothered him mildly before the incident. The owner was able to pinpoint that his anxiety seemed to worsen around the family's evening meal times when things were described as being 'a bit chaotic'. Ash is currently on treatment for arthritis and it was whilst he was at the vets for a check-up that he was referred for a behaviour consultation.

Case Study 4: Ash – Sound sensitivity. (Photo courtesy of Julie Holmes)

Significant Information

- Ash is an elderly dog and suffers from arthritis.
- The initial trigger was the pain from the spitting sausage, paired with the sound of the sizzling barbeque.
- Ash has begun to generalize the sound of the barbeque to other similar sounds including whooshing of water in the hosepipe and cooking noises associated with the preparation of meals.
- Ash is showing signs of behavioural sensitization.
- Mealtimes heighten his anxiety and are a major trigger.
- There is a young boisterous family in the home.
- We need to identify what can be used as rewards, such as favourite treats, games.

Diagnosis and Discussion

This is a good example of how a dog can make a learned association between two events (pain and a noise). As well as the hot fat burning his skin, making a hasty retreat could have jarred his arthritic joints. Clues in the history-taking were instrumental in analysing the case and it soon became clear how things developed (Fig. 11.1).

Apparently, meal times are rowdy events and it seems that the sound of the cooking, the clanging of pots and pans and the general noise from a family with three young boisterous children is causing behavioural sensitization.

Cognitive decline can cause a number of behavioural changes including an increase in anxiety and, given Ash's age, it would be worth reviewing his diet and supplementing it with antioxidants and other neurosupportive nutrients, which may help to decrease the rate of cognitive decline and aid brain function.

The BMP

Suitable training techniques

- ✓ Pattern games
- ✓ 'Hand Target' training
- ✓ 'Relax on a Mat'
- ✓ Desensitization and counter-conditioning to fear-inducing noises

DS and CC are going to be influential in Ash's treatment plan although the antecedent for most of his daily dose of anxiety is being in the kitchen at meal times.

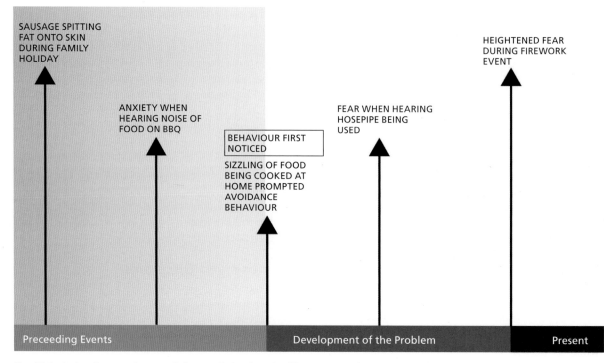

Fig. 11.1. A timeline can be a useful way of plotting significant events (*see* Chapter 7). This example, using Ash's case, demonstrates how valuable they can be in analysing a problematic behaviour.

This is the first thing to change and it is likely that, once this has been done, the owners will see an immediate improvement in his behaviour. Because of Ash's age, and his underlying arthritis, regular check-ups with the vet should be encouraged. Another aspect of this plan is providing Ash with activities that help to stimulate his brain and keep him moving to ensure his joints stay supple and free from pain.

Stage one

- Create a doggy safe space and educate the children.
- Place Ash in a relaxing environment whilst the meals are prepared (as far away as possible from the noise). During this time provide him with interactive feeders, making sure they are not too difficult but are engaging enough to keep him occupied and distracted.
- Regularly use 'Relax on a Mat' and shape relaxation.
- Perform relaxing TTouch techniques (for example ear slides).

Stage two

- 'Hand Target' training and regularly use some gentle pattern games.
- Make a list of all the things that act as triggers in preparation for DS and CC.

Stage three

- Continue with Ash's training and encourage 'seek and find' games to increase the production of dopamine (which can diminish with age).
- Once Ash's general anxiety reduces, and he is in a more relaxed state, work on DS and CC can begin. However, when working with a dog that has multiple triggers, DS and CC should begin with the least fear-inducing noise first.

Making Progress with the Plan

In my opinion, it is not necessary to work on desensitizing Ash to the general mealtime scenario. Giving him a safe and relaxing environment to retreat to, and managing his environment during meal times, is treatment in itself and, under the circumstances, is better for his welfare.

Given that the firework season is some time away, provided his anxiety is under control, DS and CC can begin in order to prepare him. However, owners must be made aware that some noise-sensitive dogs may not respond to DS and CC and can even become sensitized during the treatment. In the event that this should happen, treatment should stop with immediate effect and advice be sought from the behaviourist. Prescription medication may help and specific drugs are available from a veterinarian that can help dogs with cognitive decline.

Case Study 5: Cooper, A Three-Year-Old Male (Neutered) Wire-Haired Jack Russell Terrier

Background

Cooper belongs to a couple whose children have grown up and left home. He is highly reactive (barking, spinning and rearing up) when he sees other dogs, primarily large black ones.

Cooper was bred by a non-commercial breeder who had decided to have one litter from their own dog, as they had wanted a puppy. He has been with the current owner since he was seven weeks old and was well socialized. However, just after his vaccinations were completed, he had been taken to the puppy socialization classes at the local vets. Unfortunately, during one of the classes, a larger, black, boisterous puppy had knocked him over. Afterwards, Cooper was always reticent to mix with her and then began to bark at other larger black dogs when out on walks. Now, almost all dogs of that general description provoke a fear-aggressive response, making it impossible for the owners to go for an enjoyable walk.

They have tried numerous techniques to deal with the problem including shouting at him, rattling a can of stones to distract him and more recently have been picking him up when another dog approaches. Unfortunately, this resulted in the husband being bitten, prompting the owners to seek help.

Case Study 5: Cooper – Reactivity towards dogs. (Photo courtesy of Caroline O'Neill)

Cooper is walked on a harness with a single-clip lead on the back attachment. He enjoys his food but won't take any of his kibble on walks because he is too busy scanning his environment. He becomes alert as soon as he sees a dog approaching and this escalates as it gets closer. Cooper does however get along with a neighbour's Yorkshire Terrier and their friend's Shih Tzu.

Significant Information

- Cooper was taken away from his mother at an early age.
- Cooper experienced a frightening incident during a sensitive developmental period.
- Cooper's behaviour is specific to all larger black dogs but this could potentially generalize to dogs of all descriptions.
- Aversive methods of dealing with the problem are likely to have heightened Cooper's fear and, paired with seeing the black dog, may have exacerbated the problem.

- Cooper is regularly above threshold on his walks.
- Cooper mixes well with familiar dogs and is not yet reactive with unfamiliar small black dogs.
- Cooper's owners are using his normal food ration as treats.

Diagnosis and Discussion

There is some evidence that puppies, separated from the mother and littermates prior to eight weeks of age, experience more fearfulness on walks, reactivity to noises and have greater overall reactivity. Being picked up probably triggered the fear-potentiated startle response, which may explain his redirected aggression. Picking him up should be discouraged, not just to avoid injuries, but because in doing so, the owner may be teaching Cooper that seeing another dog is something to be concerned about. Because this problem has been developing for some time, progress will be slow but without treatment it is likely that things will worsen.

The BMP

Getting Cooper to think coherently during an episode of reactivity is unlikely, so work has to begin at home. This involves undergoing a programme of training when he is calm and receptive to learning.

Recognizing the behaviour patterns that Cooper exhibits, and knowing when to intercede, is crucial (*see* Chapter 4, Fig. 4.4). Being able to draw on suitable techniques to keep him under threshold is also critical to the plan. DS and CC should begin with small dogs (that Cooper is less reactive towards), before graduating to larger ones. Dogs with high reactivity may always have a tendency to react inappropriately under certain conditions and being observant and knowing how to manage the situation are likely to be part of Cooper's long-term plan.

Suitable training techniques

✓ Pattern games
✓ 'Muzzle Training'
✓ 'Watch Me'/'What's That?'
✓ 'Relax on a Mat'
✓ 'Come Away' and 'Emergency U-turn'
✓ 'Settle' cue
✓ Desensitization and counter-conditioning to the muzzle and to other dogs

Stage one

- Stop taking Cooper to places where he is able to rehearse his behaviour and, if possible, use a controlled environment where he can relax and enjoy his walks.
- Encourage regular meetings and play sessions with dogs that he is familiar and comfortable with.
- Identify Cooper's favourite reward. Using his daily food ration is not going to be a sufficient motivator for training.
- Stop using P+ and avoid picking him up.
- Extinguish the rearing-up behaviour by using a double-clip lead on his harness (check it has two points of contact).
- Look for opportunities to capture, mark and reward low-intensity, relaxed behaviour inside and outside the home.
- Use 'Relax on a Mat' and shape relaxation.
- Continue to teach and play pattern games.
- Continue 'Muzzle Training' and use the 'Settle' cue after sessions of play.

Stage two

Generalize his training to slightly more distracting environments:

- 'Emergency U-turn'
- 'Come Away'
- 'Watch Me'/'What's That?'
- Based on Cooper's history, establish the critical distance in preparation for work on DS and CC techniques

Stage three

- Enlisting a helper who has an unfamiliar but friendly small, dark-coated 'stooge' dog, means work on DS and CC can proceed.
- The environment used should be spacious and controlled and, similar to Zak's BMP plan, using a mobile phone will help to ensure that the criteria for moving closer can be discussed.
- Mark and reward low-intensity behaviour.
- Keeping Cooper on a long-line, at a safe distance means that these staged meetings are under control.

- If Cooper is relaxed with the smaller dog, and it is safe to do so (as he is muzzled), the long-lines can be dropped so they can interact more naturally.
- Progress can gradually be made using slightly larger, unfamiliar dogs.

Making Progress with the Plan

DS and CC training can progress, gradually introducing Cooper to medium-sized, darker-coloured dogs and, over time, slowly increasing their size. This should follow a similar pattern to the work already carried out but progress is bound to be slower and going back in the stages of training is a strong possibility.

Finding 'stooge' dogs can be limiting but working with a trainer who is able to provide friendly dogs may be possible. Manikins might be another alternative and, at a distance, they can be effective. Cooper's case, Like Zak's (and Holly's), is well suited to BAT training techniques and the principles can be easily integrated into his plan.

End Note

Although this book is by no means a complete guide, I do hope that it has left you with more answers than questions. My main endeavour has been to help you understand your dog and to provide you with some useful, practical management tools and techniques so that you feel better equipped to help them lead a happier life.

With knowledge comes confidence and this is often the key to supporting a fearful and anxious dog.

I wish you and your dog the best of luck in your training journey together, but do remember that if you have any concerns to always consult a veterinary surgeon, canine behaviourist or dog trainer.

Further Resources

Suggested Reading List

Behavior Adjustment Training in Dogs by Grisha Stewart (Dogwise Publishing, 2012)

Controlled Unleashed: Creating a Focused and Confident Dog by Leslie McDevitt (Clean Run Productions, 2007)

Dog Food Logic by Linda P. Case (Dogwise Publishing, 2014)

Doggie Language: A Dog Lover's Guide to Understanding Your Best Friend by Lili Chin (Summersdale Publishers Limited, 2020)

Fearful to Fear Free by M. Becker, L. Radosta, W. Sung and M. Becker (Health Communications Incorporated, 2018)

Feisty Fido: Help for the Leash-Reactive Dog by P.B. McConnell and K.B. London (McConnell Publishing Limited, 2003)

Good Dog: The Easy Way to Train Your Dog by Sarah Whitehead (Collins & Brown, 2011)

How Dogs Learn by Mary R. Burch and Jon S. Bailey (Wiley Publishing, 1999)

Inside of a Dog: What Dogs See, Smell, and Know by Alexandra Horowitz (Simon & Schuster, 2012)

Life-skills for Puppies: Laying the foundation for a loving, lasting relationship by H. Zulch, D. Mills and P. Baumber (Hubble and Hattie, 2018)

On Talking Terms with Dogs: Calming Signals by Turid Rugaas (Dogwise Publishing, 2005)

Separation Anxiety in Dogs: Next Generation Treatment Protocols and Practices by Malena DeMartini-Price (Dogwise Publishing, 2020)

The Cautious Canine: How to Help Dogs Conquer Their Fears by P.B. McConnell (McConnell Publishing, 2009)

The Puppy Primer by B. Scidmore and P.B. McConnell (McConnell Publishing Limited, 2010)

WAG – The Science of Making Your Dog Happy by Zazie Todd (Greystone Books Limited, 2020)

Your End of the Lead: Changing how you think and act to help your reactive dog by Janet Finlay (Independently published, 2019)

Useful Resources

Finding a Behaviour Counsellor/Dog Trainer

Anyone can call themselves an animal behaviourist or dog trainer. However, without the relevant theoretical and practical knowledge, much harm can be done. Therefore, to ensure you get the right kind of help, any of the following organizations can be relied upon to guide you to a suitably qualified behaviour practitioner and dog trainer in the area where you live.

Behaviour Counsellors

- Animal Behaviour and Training Council register of behaviourists: www.abtcouncil.org.uk/index/abtc-members-by-region.html
- Association of Pet Behaviour Counsellors (APBC): www.apbc.org.uk
- Association for the Study of Animal Behaviour (ASAB) register of certified clinical animal behaviourists: www.asab.org/ccab-register
- Fellowship of Animal Behaviour Clinicians (FAB Clinicians): www.fabclinicians.org
- The International Association of Animal Behavior Consultants (IAABC): m.iaabc.org

Dog Trainers

- Animal Behaviour and Training Council register of trainers and behaviourists: www.abtcouncil.org.uk/index/abtc-members-by-region.html
- The Association of Pet Dog Trainers (APDT): www.apdt.co.uk

Useful Websites

Animal Centred Education: www.animalcentrededucation.com

Association of British Veterinary Acupuncturists: www.abva.co.uk

Breakthrough Diet: www.breakthroughdog.co.uk

British Association of Homeopathic Veterinary Surgeons: www.bahvs.com

British Association of Veterinary Herbalists: www.herbalvets.org.uk

Clicker training: www.clickertraining.com

Dog appeasing pheromone products: www.adaptil.com/uk

Dogs Trust (free sound effects): www.dogstrust.org.uk/help-advice/dog-behaviour-health/sound-therapy-for-pets

Fear Free Happy Homes: www.fearfreehappyhomes.com

Mantrailing: www.mantrailinguk.com

Tellington Touch: www.ttouch.com

The Puppy Contract: www.puppycontract.org.uk

The Yellow Dog Project: www.yellowdoguk.co.uk

Bibliography

Chapter 1

Bowen, J. and Heath, S., *Behaviour Problems in Small Animals: Practical Advice for the Veterinary Team* (Elsevier, 2005)

de Assis, L.S., Matos, R., Pike, T.W., Burman, O.H.P. and Mills, D.S., 'Developing Diagnostic Frameworks in Veterinary Behavioral Medicine: Disambiguating Separation Related Problems in Dogs.' *Front Vet Science* (January 2020)

DeMartini-Price, M., *Treating Separation Anxiety in Dogs* (Dogwise Publishing, 2014)

Kubo, K.Y., Iinuma, M. and Chen, H., 'Mastication as a Stress-Coping Behavior', *Biomed Research International* (May 2015)

Leon, M., Rosado, M., García-Belenguerb, S., Chacon, G., Villegasb, A. and Palaciob, J., 'Assessment of serotonin in serum, plasma, and platelets of aggressive dogs'. *Journal of Veterinary Behavior: Clinical Applications and Research* (2012)

Chapter 2

Asher, L., England, G.C.W., Sommerville, R. and Harvey, N.D., 'Teenage dogs? Evidence for adolescent-phase conflict behaviour and an association between attachment to humans and pubertal timing in the domestic dog'. In *Biol Lett.* 16 (5) (2020)

Becker, M., Radosta, L., Sung, W. and Becker, M., *Fearful to Fear Free* (Health Communications Incorporated, 2018)

Dias, B.G. and Ressler, K.J., 'Parental olfactory experience influences behavior and neural structure in subsequent generations', *Nature Neuroscience* (2014, pp. 89–96)

Dietz, L., Arnold, A.K., Goerlich, V.C. and Vinke, C.M., 'The importance of early life experiences for the development of behavioural disorders in domestic dogs', *Behaviour* (2018, pp. 83–114)

Foyer, P., Wilsson, E. and Jensen, P., 'Levels of maternal care in dogs affect adult offspring temperament', *Science Reports* (2016, pp. 1-32)

Gazzano, A., Mariti, C., Notari, L., Sighieri, C. and McBride, E.A., 'Effects of early gentling and early environment on emotional development of puppies', *Applied Animal Behaviour Science* (2008, pp. 294–304)

Herron, M.E., Shofer, F.S. and Reisner, I.R., 'Survey of the use and outcome of confrontational and non-confrontational training methods in client-owned dogs showing undesired behaviors', *Applied Animal Behaviour Science* (2009, pp. 47–54)

Mills, D. *et al.*, 'Pain and Problem Behavior in Cats and Dogs', *Animals, volume 10 issue 2* (February 2020), accessed from https://www.mdpi.com

Morrow, M., Ottobre, J., Ottobre, A., Neville, P., St-Pierre, N., Dreschel, N. and Pate, J., 'Breed-Dependent Differences in the Onset of Fear-Related Avoidance Behavior in Puppies', *Journal of Veterinary Behavior* (August 2015, pp. 286–294)

Overall, K.L., *Manual of Clinical Behavioral Medicine for Dogs and Cats* (Elsevier, 2013)

Scidmore, B. and McConnell, P.B., *The Puppy Primer* (McConnell Publishing Limited, 2010)

Todd, Z., *WAG: The Science of Making Your Dog Happy* (Greystone Books Limited, 2020)

Vieira de Castro, A.C., Fuchs, V., Gabriela, M.M., Pastur, S., de Sousa, L. and Olsson, A.S., 'Does training method matter? Evidence for the negative impact of aversive-based methods on companion dog welfare', *PLoS One 15 no 12* (Dec 2020) Accessed from https://journals.plos.org/

Chapter 3

Bowen, J. and Heath, S., '*Meanings of Different Canine Vocalisations', Behaviour Problems in Small Animals: Practical Advice for the Veterinary Team* (Elsevier, 2005)

D'Aniello, B., Semin, G.R., Alterisio, A., Aria, M., and Scandurra, A., 'Interspecies transmission of emotional information via chemosignals: From human to dogs (*Canis Lupus Familiaris*)' *Animal Cognition* (January 2018, pp. 67–78)

Grigg, E.K., Chou, J., Parker, E., Gatesy-Davis, A., Clarkson, S.T. and Hart, L.A., 'Stress-Related Behaviors in Companion Dogs Exposed to Common Household Noises, and Owners' Interpretations of Their Dogs' Behaviors', *Frontiers in Veterinary Science* (November 2021) Accessed from https://www.frontiersin.org/

Horowitz, A., Inside of a Dog: What Dogs See, Smell, and Know (Simon & Schuster, 2012)

Overall, K.L., *Manual of Clinical Behavioral Medicine for Dogs and Cats* (Elsevier, 2013)

Siniscalchi. M., Lusito, R., Vallortigara, G. and Quaranta, A., 'Seeing left- or right-asymmetric tail wagging produces different emotional responses in dogs', *Current Biology* (November 2013, pp. 2279–2282)

Chapter 4

McPeake, K.J., Collins, L.M., Zulch, H. and Mills, D.S., 'The Canine Frustration Questionnaire: Development of a New Psychometric Tool for Measuring Frustration in Domestic Dogs (*Canis familiaris*)', *Frontiers in Veterinary Science* (May 2019) Accessed from https://www.frontiersin.org/

Overall, K.L., *Manual of Clinical Behavioral Medicine for Dogs and Cats* (Elsevier, 2013)

Warnes, C., 'Five myths commonly associated with neutering in dogs', *The Veterinary Nurse* (November 2014, pp. 502–508)

Chapter 5

Becker, M., Radosta, L., Sung, W. and Becker, M., *Fearful to Fear Free* (Health Communications Incorporated, 2018)

Dinwoodie, I.R., Zottola, V. and Dodman, N.H., 'An Investigation into the Impact of Pre-Adolescent Training on Canine Behavior', *Animals* (April 2021) Accessed from https://www.mdpi.com/

Marti, C., Gazzano, A., Lansdown Moore, J., Baragli, P., Chelli, L. and Sighieri, C., 'Perception of dogs' stress by their owners', *Journal of Veterinary Behavior: Clinical Applications and Research* (2012, pp. 213–219)

McMillan, F.D., 'Behavioral and psychological outcomes for dogs sold as puppies through pet stores and/or born in commercial breeding establishments: Current knowledge and putative causes', *Journal of Veterinary Behavior* (May–June 2017, pp. 14–26)

Chapter 6

Burch, M. and Bailey, J., *How Dogs Learn* (Wiley Publishing Incorporated, 1999)

Todd, Z., *WAG: The Science of Making Your Dog Happy* (Greystone Books Limited, 2020)

Chapter 7

Friedman, S.G., 'Functional Assessment: Hypothesizing predictors and purposes of problem behaviour to improve behaviour change plans'. Paper presented to the annual conference of the North American Veterinary conference, Orlando FL. (Jan 2009) accessed online 26.2.2021

Overall, K.L., 'Understanding how dogs learn in training and behaviour modification', World Small Animal Veterinary Association Congress, proceedings (2006) accessed online 27.12.2021

Chapter 8

Affenzeller, N., Palme, R. and Zulch, H., 'Playful activity post-learning improves training performance in Labrador Retriever dogs (*Canis lupus familiaris*)', *Physiology & Behavior* (October 2016 pp. 62–73)

McConnell, P.B. and London, K.B., *Feisty Fido: Help for the Leash-Reactive Dog* (McConnell Publishing Limited, 2003)

McDevitt, L., *Controlled Unleashed: Creating a Focused and Confident Dog* (Clean Run Productions 2003)

Stewart, G., *Behavior Adjustment Training* (Dogwise Publishing, 2012)

Chapter 9

Graham, L., Wells, D.L. and Hepper, P., 'The influence of olfactory stimulation on the behaviour of dogs housed in a rescue shelter', *Applied Animal Behaviour Science* (May 2005, pp. 143–153)

King, C., Buffington, L., Smith, T.J. and Grandin, T., 'The effect of a pressure wrap (Thundershirt) on heart rate and behavior in canines diagnosed with anxiety disorder', *The Journal of Veterinary Science* (October 2014, pp. 215–221)

McGowan, R.T.S., Barnett, H.R., Czarnecki-Maulden, G.L., Si, X., Perez-Camargo, G., and Martin, F., 'Tapping into those "gut feelings": Impact of BL999 (*Bifidobacterium longum*) on anxiety in dogs', *Veterinary Behavior Symposium Proceedings, Denver,* (July 2018, pp. 8–9)

Scott, S., 'Complementary, alternative and integrated therapies', *BSAVA Canine and Feline Behavioural Medicine*, Ed. Horowitz, D., Mills, D.S., and Heath, S., (2002 BSAVA, pp. 249–255)

Wells, D.L., 'Aromatherapy for travel-induced excitement in dogs', *Journal of the American Veterinary Medical Association* (2006, pp. 964–7)

Chapter 10

McConnell, P.B. and London, K.B., *Feisty Fido: Help for the Leash-Reactive Dog* (McConnell Publishing Limited, 2003)

Bowen, J. and Heath, S., *Behaviour Problems in Small Animals: Practical Advice for the Veterinary Team* (Elsevier, 2005)

Chapter 11

Pierantoni, L., Albertini, M. and Pirrone, F., 'Prevalence of owner reported behaviours in dogs separated from the litters at two different ages', *Veterinary Record* (October 2011 pp. 468)

DeMartini-Price, M., *Treating Separation Anxiety in Dogs* (Dogwise Publishing, 2014)

Glossary

Acute – Sudden and short-lived.

Affiliative – Friendly, peaceful acts exchanged between individuals.

Agonistic – Being aggressive or defensive.

Amino acids – Molecules that combine to form proteins.

Anatomy – The science of the structure of the body.

Antecedents – Events, situations, or conditions that precede the behaviour.

Antioxidants – Natural or man-made substances that prevent or delay damage to cells.

Appeasement – A form of behaviour in which one individual attempts, through submissive displays, to avoid injury or conflict.

Approach-avoidance conflict – When there is one goal or event that has positive and negative effects that make the goal both appealing and unappealing at the same time.

Approximations – Small progressive steps that lead to the behavioural goal. Used in 'shaping'.

Arousal/aroused – In behaviour relates to being physiologically alert or attentive.

Arthritis – Inflammation of the joints.

Aversive – Unpleasant.

Chronic – Lasting and enduring.

Classical conditioning – A form of associative learning when two stimuli are linked together to produce a new learned response.

Cognition/cognitive – The process of gaining knowledge and understanding through thought, experience, and the senses.

Conditioning/conditioned – Pertains to learning. The reaction (or response) to an object or event (stimulus) can be modified by learning or conditioning. The two main classes of learning are operant conditioning and classical conditioning.

Counter-conditioning – The process of learning a new response which is different and incompatible with the previously learned, undesirable response.

Cues – Antecedents that we teach.

Desensitization – The gradual exposure to aversive stimuli at a level where there is no negative response. Eventually the dog can tolerate the stimulus without exhibiting the undesirable response.

Dilated – To make it wider.

Endocrine gland – A ductless gland that produces a hormone carried in the bloodstream targeting a specific organ or body-system, for example. thyroid, pancreas.

Epigenetics – The study of changes in organisms caused by modification of gene expression rather than alteration of the genetic code itself.

Extinction – The weakening of a behaviour when it is no longer reinforced.

Extinguish – To put an end to a behaviour using the principles of extinction.

Generalization – In behaviour, this is when an individual responds in the same way to different but similar stimuli.

Genetics – A branch of biology that deals with the heredity and variation of organisms.

Habituation – A decrease in response to a stimulus after repeated presentations. The opposite to sensitization.

Heredity – The biological processes by which particular characteristics are transmitted from parents to their offspring.

Hormone – A chemical substance that excites activity.

Innate – Inborn behaviour.

In-utero – Within the uterus (womb).

Neuroscience – The science and study of the brain and nervous system, especially in relation to behaviour and learning.

Neurotransmitter – Chemical molecules used by the nervous system to transmit messages between neurons, or from neurons to muscles.

One-event learning – A single incident that is (or is perceived to be) so traumatic that it causes a lasting memory of that event.

Operant conditioning – A procedure that makes a response more or less likely as a result of its consequences.

Pharmacology – A branch of medicine relating to the uses, effects and modes of action of drugs.

Physiology – Relates to the normal functions of living organisms and their parts.

Precursor – Component from which another substance or cellular component is formed.

Prognosis – The expected course or outcome of a condition.

Puberty – The phase when an animal becomes reproductively mature.

Reinforcer – A stimulus which, when presented following a behavioural response, increases the probability of that behaviour being repeated.

Respiratory rate – The rate at which breathing occurs. This is usually measured in breaths per minute. The normal resting rate in dogs is ten to 30 thirty breaths per minute.

Sensitization (behavioural) – In contrast to habituation, sensitization causes a more exaggerated response to a stimulus with repeated exposure.

Stimulus (singular)/stimuli (plural) – Some thing or things that provoke or cause an action or response.

Stressor – A stimulus that causes a stress response.

Stooge – In dog training is a calm, quiet, sensible dog or person that keeps within a critical distance to help in the process of desensitizing and counter-conditioning a dog.

Temperament – The biologically determined behavioural characteristics and tendencies that a dog is born with and which are consistent over time.

Acknowledgements

Writing a book can be a lonely experience and reaching out to ask people for help isn't always easy. Everyone is busy and you don't want to impose on them. However, I wouldn't have been able to finish the book without the support of some special people.

First of all, I would like to thank my husband, Phil, who spent endless hours proof reading through it and acting as a sound-board. In addition to taking the brunt of my emotional outbursts during moments of self-doubt, he also held things together in the running of the home whilst I spent an inordinate amount of time in front of the computer.

Joanne Tarling was also there for me. She always has been – ever since we were young girls working together as veterinary nurses back in the eighties. Joanne didn't need any asking and kindly offered to read every chapter, giving me some really valuable feedback and cheering me on along the way. Thank you, Joanne.

Tommy Taylor is a creative genius. I really don't know how I could have completed the book without his help. He's responsible for bringing my ideas together in the illustrations that are peppered throughout it and took some amazing photographs too. He also helped with everything IT, which was an immense relief as it isn't my strong point! On top of all that, he kept things running smoothly with my business, taking care of enquiries and making sure the website was working as it should be. He's always given his time generously and spent long days helping me meet the deadline. On top of all that, he's a valued friend and I feel very lucky to have him in my life.

A special thank you also goes to Dr Marianne Dorn (Rehab Vet), a veterinary surgeon and physiotherapist who kindly gave her time and expertise freely. Also, my thanks to fellow behaviourists Hannah Donovan-Calam, Gretta Ford, Claire Klima, Rosie Myers, Christine Spencer, Jo Whitehead and Nikki Wilson for their wisdom and experience.

As the saying goes, 'a picture is worth a thousand words'. They feature heavily in this book and bring it to life, so I'd like to express my gratitude to everyone who took the time to share pictures of their dogs with me. Looking through them has given me hours of pleasure. The requirements for reproduction in a book are exacting, so apologies to those people whose photographs didn't get used. I still loved seeing them.

Sincere thanks are also in order to Crowood for editorial direction and advice and to the Association of Pet Behaviour Counsellors (APBC), an amazing organization that is so supportive of its members (of which I am one) and champions the welfare of animals.

Last, but by no means least, are the wonderful dogs that I have had the pleasure of helping and who have taught me so much. Of course, this has only been made possible by the veterinary surgeons who have referred cases and the owners who have entrusted their dog's care to me. Without them, I wouldn't have been able to write the book.

Index